UNFAIR ADVANTAGE

Copyright © 2014 by Garrett Milovich

All rights reserved. Written permission must be secured from the publisher to use or reproduce any part of this book, except for brief quotations in critical reviews or articles.

Unless otherwise noted, Scripture quotations are from THE NEW KING JAMES VERSION. Copyright © 1979, 1980, 1982, 1990, 1994 by Thomas Nelson, Inc.

For Cheyne

Table of Contents

INTRODUCTION: I Am Batman
vii

CHAPTER 1: Why Am I Here?
1

CHAPTER 2: World's Best Dad
15

CHAPTER 3: Why Do You Call Me Good?
29

CHAPTER 4: The New You
43

CHAPTER 5: Like God
59

CHAPTER 6: The Dream House
73

CHAPTER 7: Great Expectations
87

CHAPTER 8: Greater Expectations
105

CHAPTER 9: Worthy
121

CHAPTER 10: My Least Favorite Bible Story
139

CHAPTER 11: Change the World
157

CHAPTER 12: Kings or Priests
173

EPILOGUE: Go
183

*But God, who is rich in mercy, because of
His great love with which He loved us,
even when we were dead in our trespasses,
made us alive together with Christ
(by grace you have been saved).*

Ephesians 2:4-5

Introduction
I Am Batman

How would your life be different if you knew you couldn't fail?

Think about it. Would you speak differently? Would you think differently? Would you *dress* differently? What about your career? You may be sitting in an office chair as you read this. Is that where you'd be sitting if you knew you couldn't lose? Would your hobbies change? Would your personality change? Would your friends change? Would your church change? Would things be *any* different if you honestly believed you were destined to win in life?

Well, if you've made Jesus Christ the Lord of your life, then I have some great news for you: you are destined to win.

Hold on. I think a statement like that warrants at least *some* excitement from us, so let me say it again, this time with proper emphasis:

YOU ARE ABSOLUTELY DESTINED TO WIN!!!

Much better.

You see, we all have a specific calling in this life. As the "Body of Christ," each of us plays a vital role in this story, an irreplaceable piece in this puzzle called Life. I'm reminded of the story of Saul's conversion. As Saul is traveling along the road to Damascus, hell-bent on squashing the explosive growth of a new Jewish cult of fishermen called "Christianity," Jesus Himself, in all His glory, materializes before Saul's eyes, plucking him out of a lifetime of empty religion and converting him to the truth. Saul is blinded by the light, and Jesus sends him into the city to await further instruction.

Most of us remember that part of the story. But the true hero of the story is a man by the name of Ananias.

> "Now there was a certain disciple at Damascus named Ananias; and to him the Lord said in a vision, 'Ananias.' And he said, 'Here I am, Lord.' So the Lord said to him, 'Arise and go to the street called Straight, and inquire at the house of Judas for one called Saul of Tarsus, for behold, he is praying. And in a vision he has seen a man named Ananias coming in and putting his hand on him, so that he might receive his sight.'" (Acts 9:10-12)

I find this part of the story utterly fascinating. Saul's healing and subsequent maturity in the things of God is contingent on Ananias' obedience to God's command. Jesus told Saul to expect a man named Ananias to show up *before* Ananias even agreed to go. What if Ananias had said "no"? What if he wasn't listening that day? Look at the unwavering confidence that Jesus placed in Ananias.

Jesus trusted Ananias so much that he committed him to go and serve Saul before even speaking to him about it. I mean, what would the newly converted Saul think if Ananias didn't show up? It's not like there were tons of committed Christians named "Ananias" at this point. There was only one other guy named Ananias, and he was kind of a jerk. He was also dead (Acts 5). What would God have done if Ananias was too dense to obey?

"Hey, Saul. Jesus sent me to heal you."

Blind Saul looks up. "Oh, great! You must be Ananias."

The man looks at him awkwardly. "Um, actually, no," he says. "I'm Jeff."

A baffled expression washes over Saul's face. "I thought… I'm pretty sure Jesus said your name would be Ananias."

"Yeah, well, the thing is... Ananias was busy. His mom just bought him Assassin's Creed. But do not fear, for I, Jeff, am here!"

And so it was that Saul began to question whether Jesus was indeed the Almighty God of the Universe.

But alas, this cumbersome conversation was unnecessary because Ananias was prepared to accept his divine destiny. I don't know if Ananias would qualify as a kneecap, a finger, or a tendon in Christ's body, but whatever part he was, he performed it with excellence and changed the world. For if Saul had not been set on the path to someday become the mighty apostle Paul, author of thirteen New Testament epistles, teacher of Luke, and founder of a plethora of churches, who knows what the world would be like today. The New Testament would be significantly shorter, much of the church would still be in bondage under the law... in fact, would there even be a church today?

We all have a role to play as this divine romance unfolds. And my job is this: to teach Christians who God has made them to be, so that they are equipped to do the work that God has called them to do. I struggled with this calling for many years. My heart burns for evangelism. It is an almost obsessive passion for me. I want to see the lost reached and the dying saved. But it's not my job. My job is to prepare others, to prepare you, to step into God's plan for your life. And you cannot do that if you don't know who you are. Let me say that again. *You cannot effectively serve God if you don't know who you are.*

Right now, there are future pastors reading this book. There are evangelists reading it, too. Apostles, prophets, teachers. Sunday school volunteers, deacons, ushers, worship leaders. And not just church employees. There are bankers, engineers, truck drivers, students, and many, many others. And it is of the utmost importance that you understand who you are *in Christ*. No matter the call, no matter the destiny, recognizing who God has made you to be will cause you to fulfill that destiny, to accomplish the task, to *win*.

God has given you an *Unfair Advantage* in life.

Look at the great superheroes that adorn the big screens. Batman scours the streets of Gotham, fighting injustice, vanquishing evil, and saving his city. How is he able to do it? He doesn't have any special powers, any magic spider bites, any extraterrestrial heritage. How does he find the time? Why doesn't he need a job like the rest of us?

Simple. He has a *huge* inheritance left to him by his parents. He's not stuck at a nine-to-five because he's loaded. His utility belt is crammed with nifty gadgets that he didn't have to work for. He drives a car that was purchased with his parents' cash. No one else could have been Batman. It's actually pretty unfair when you think about it. His relationship with his parents gave him an edge in life that allowed him to do great things.

You, too, have a rich Parent.

> *"And my God shall supply all your need according to His riches in glory by Christ Jesus."* (Philippians 4:19)

> *"And God is able to make all grace abound toward you, that you, always having all sufficiency in all things, may have an abundance for every good work."* (2 Corinthians 9:8)

My Dad's not just rich; He's *loaded*. Oh, you would not believe how much Holy Spirit joy I experienced when I found out I was Batman!

Superman is essentially a god among men. He's faster than a speeding bullet, more powerful than a locomotive. And it seems he has a new superpower every week. Is there anything he can't do?

> *"I can do all things through Christ who strengthens me."* (Philippians 4:13)

His dad isn't human, making him fundamentally different from everyone around him. Sure, he lives here, but this isn't his home.

> "They are not of the world, just as I am not of the world." (John 17:16)

> "For our citizenship is in heaven…" (Philippians 3:20)

With the exception of kryptonite, is there anything that can kill him? Punch him, kick him, strangle him, stab him, shoot him, crush him, run him over, blow him up… the guy is indestructible.

> "No weapon formed against you shall prosper…" (Isaiah 54:17)

> "'Behold, I give you authority to trample on serpents and scorpions, and over all the power of the enemy, and nothing shall by any means hurt you.'" (Luke 10:19)

Kal-El, the last son of Krypton, was saved from the imminent destruction of his former world.

> "And you He made alive, who were dead in trespasses and sins." (Ephesians 2:1)

And after his salvation, it became apparent that his greater destiny lay in helping those around him, in saving the lost from a fallen world.

> "'Heal the sick, cleanse the lepers, raise the dead, cast out demons. Freely you have received, freely give.'" (Matthew 10:8)

> "And He said to them, 'Go into all the world and preach the gospel to every living creature.'" (Mark 16:15)

You would not believe the inexplicable bliss that consumed my soul when I discovered I was Superman!

Think of David. Consider the steadfast confidence he exudes as he stands before Goliath. The speech he gives on the battlefield that day, with thousands of terrified Israelites and thousands of arrogant Philistines in attendance, puts William Wallace's *Freedom* speech from *Braveheart* to shame:

> "'You come to me with a sword, with a spear, and with a javelin. But I come to you in the name of the Lord of hosts, the God of the armies of Israel, whom you have defied. This day the Lord <u>will</u> deliver you into my hand, and I will strike you and take your head from you. And this day I will give the carcasses of the camp of the Philistines to the birds of the air and the wild beasts of the earth, that all the earth may know that there is a God in Israel. Then all this assembly shall know that the Lord does not save with a sword and spear; for the battle is the Lord's, and He <u>will</u> give you into our hands.'" (1 Samuel 17:45-47)

There was no fear. No questioning. Just confidence. Just *faith*. He knew his God. He knew his power. He had an unfair advantage, and he knew it.

Remember those three Jewish boys, hundreds of miles away from home in a country not their own:

> "'If [you throw us into the furnace], our God whom we serve is able to deliver us from the burning fiery furnace, and He <u>will</u> deliver us from your hand, O king. But if [you don't throw us into the furnace], let it be known to you, O king, that we do not serve your gods, nor will we worship the gold image you have set up." (Daniel 3:17-18)

They had an unfair advantage, and they knew it. In fact, it seems that *all* the mighty men and women of God had this in common. Moses, Abraham, Elijah, Elisha, Peter, Paul… they knew who God was, and they knew that as long as they stuck with God,

He'd always have their back. They all had an unfair advantage in life.

Think of Jesus. Surely Jesus had this unfair advantage in life. He went head to head with satan many a time, and always came out on top. He cast out demons. He opened blind eyes. He cured leprosy. He made the lame walk. He turned water to wine. He multiplied fish. He walked on water. He outsmarted Pharisees. He liberated slaves. He raised the dead. He died Himself, and yet still somehow came back to life. He redeemed a lost world. He brought hope to billions of people who by definition were without hope. He walked with God.

Jesus is the greatest of them all.

> *"'Most assuredly, I say to you, he who believes in Me, the works that I do he will do also; and greater works than these he will do, because I go to My Father.'" (John 14:12)*

You have an unfair advantage in life. You are greater than you realize. The devil doesn't stand a chance.

1
Why Am I Here?

Wait. Why am I here?

Once again, I found myself in the kitchen. As embarrassing as it is, this happens a lot.

Okay. I just ate lunch, so I know I'm not hungry. At least, I don't feel *hungry.*

I work at a traffic engineering firm in Irvine, California. Our headquarters is essentially a long, skinny hallway with rooms on either side. My office is at the front end of the hallway; at the other end is the copy room, printer, office supplies, reference books, and of course, the kitchen.

Did I print something… no, I don't think so… maybe I – no, that's not it…

Suddenly, it occurs to me that I've been standing in the kitchen doorway for upwards of thirty seconds. Self consciousness sweeps in, and I find myself very concerned with what everyone else is thinking. I know for a fact that Shane's desk is pointed straight in my direction.

Make a decision, Garrett! Either go into the kitchen and grab a banana, or head back to your office. This is crunch time!

I start to head back to my office.

Whatever it was, it'll still be there when you get back to your office.

You'll figure it out then.

I stop dead in my tracks. It's approximately 150 feet back to my office. I know. I've counted. I'm an engineer.

One hundred and fifty feet back to my office? Plus, one hundred and fifty feet to walk back *here to get whatever the heck it is I'm looking for. Then, one hundred and fifty feet* back *to my office. That's four hundred and fifty feet! That's almost a* tenth *of a mile!*

I stop myself from doing mental math before I factor in average walking speeds, friction coefficients, wind resistance, drag, and whatever other meaningless mathematical factors I could throw into the equation to overcomplicate it even more. Did I mention I'm an engineer?

I *was* standing in the kitchen, wondering why I was there. Now, I'm seven feet from the kitchen, wondering if Bernoulli's Principle applies to my current predicament. It's not much of an upgrade, so I quickly duck into the closest shelter I can find: the copy room. Finally safe from the judging eyes of the twenty civil engineers that staff our company, I can pause and figure out why I'm there.

As I step into the copy room, I spot a brightly adorned autoCAD printout waiting for me at the copier. Sudden clarity sweeps in and slaps me across the face. I sheepishly grab the sheet, and begin my 150-foot trek back to my desk.

Right now, there are over seven billion people on the planet, and as funny as it sounds, I think this story is a very appropriate description of their day to day lives.

The Question of the Ages

Why am I here?

Since the dawn of mankind, our unique race has been trying to figure out the answer to this question. For a long time, man believed we were simply chess pieces, being sporadically and often irrationally flung around by the likes of Zeus and his Greek cohorts with or without our consent. In other parts of the world, popular consensus maintains that we are the subconscious wonderings of Brahma, Buddha, Vishnu, Krishna, or any other of a long list of enlightened deities. For those who consider themselves more educated than the church, we are supposedly the long and laborious result of a random yet guided process known as evolution, slowly adapting from pond scum to reptile to mammal to, well, us. They'd say there's no rhyme or reason to why we are here, so just live it up and enjoy.

Why am I here?

The church has debated this issue since its inception, and I'm still shocked by the lack of a cohesive answer. This is quite troubling, since as any traveler will tell you, *If you don't know where you came from, you can't possibly know where you are going.*

One group of Christians will say that we were created to get people saved. While it's true that we *are* indeed supposed to get people saved, that doesn't really answer WHY we are here. It more answers the question, WHAT NOW? After all, if God simply wanted people to go street-witnessing, why make people in the first place? And why continue making people? Also, consider that in the Garden of Eden, Adam and Eve *were* saved. God had two saved individuals, and no one for them to witness to. Mission accomplished! Well done, good and faithful servant! No need for additional people, unless God is more concerned with a convoluted game of chess than He is with us, which sadly enough, is what many Christians believe about our Heavenly Father.

Another group claims that we were created for the sole purpose of worshiping God. Again, this can sound deceptively convincing, because we *are* supposed to worship God. But while God is amazing and incredible and powerful and holy and good and certainly worthy of our praise and adoration, that is not why God created us. I mean, think that through for a second. Eons ago, before the creation of the heavens and the earth, God leans over to

Jesus and says, "You know what, Son? We're pretty great."

"We certainly are, Dad," says Jesus.

"But how can We be sure," the Holy Spirit chimes in, "unless we have someone to constantly assure us?"

"Good point!" God says. "Jesus, can You take care of that?"

"Already on it, Dad," Jesus responds as He walks out of the garage with His tool box.

Is that the true story of Genesis, the "Behind the Scenes" account of Creation, the legendary Beginning? Is that really the God that we serve? One desperate for our worship, incessantly needy of our approval?

Don't get me wrong. There is nothing as sweet as the presence of God. And we are certainly *supposed* to worship God. Spending time in the presence of God, giving voice to my love and adoration of my Savior King, is actually one of my favorite pastimes. But it is very apparent that worship is not the reason God made us. If that were all He was after, He would have stopped after forming the angels (whose job is to worship God *and* serve these peculiar creatures called "humans").

The church has been attempting to answer this question for thousands of years, but it seems apparent to me that the church has failed miserably. So again, I ask you:

Why are we here?

The Answer We've Been Looking For

The answer is incredibly simple, actually. In fact, you will find the meaning of your existence throughout the entirety of scripture. Let's start in the gospel of Luke.

> *"Now Jesus Himself began His ministry at about thirty years of age, being (as was supposed) the son of Joseph, the son of Heli... the son of Enosh, the son of Seth, the son of Adam, the son of God." (Luke 3:23, 38)*

Did you see it? Adam isn't called the servant of God. He's not referred to as the messenger of God, nor is he the worship leader of God, the errand-boy of God, or God's lackey. Adam is *God's son*. The reason God made Adam was because He wanted a family. Not a company or a ministry. *A family.* I find this astoundingly beautiful. As I'm typing this right now, just thinking about the fact that God made me to be a part of His family is causing me to laugh out loud. God is so incredibly good!

Think about most families nowadays. Why do people start having kids? Yes, there are those who procreate to manipulate their family, friends, and the IRS, but ignoring those extreme outliers, why do couples typically start a family? My wife and I have been talking about having kids this year. My reasons for wanting a child do not include "so they can help with chores." Also not included on that list are things like "so they can affirm that I am a great father" or "so I can control every part of their lives."

The reason you were put on this earth isn't so you could sing praise and worship songs to God (although that is something you should do). It's also not to tell the world about Jesus (although that is something you should do). It's not even so that you can direct your love towards God (although that is something you should do). On the contrary, you are here so that *God can direct His love toward you*. You were meant to be the object of God's affection, His companionship, *His love*.

This becomes quite apparent when you look at God's interactions with people throughout the entire scope of human history. Genesis tells us that immediately after God created Adam and Eve,

> *"...God blessed them, and God said to them, 'Be fruitful and multiply; fill the earth and subdue it; have dominion over the fish of the sea, over the birds of the air, and over every living thing that moves on the earth.'" (Genesis 1:28)*

The first thing God does after the birth of His son and daughter is He blesses them. Now, it's easy for Christians to hear words without really knowing what they mean. "Bless" is one of those words that Christians will often read, hear, and use, without a decent understanding of what it actually means. The word translated here as *Bless* is the Hebrew word "barak," which means *"to bless, to salute, to adore."*

Picture the scene that unravels in this passage of scripture. God has just spent six days forming the entire universe (my mouth falls open just thinking of it). Countless waves crashing upon countless beaches, millions of trees that sprung from the earth in a matter of seconds, birds flying over vast plains, sunsets that somehow manage to perfectly blend every last color, colors (after all, He could've created the heavens and the earth in black-and-white), billions upon billions of stars. Simply put, creation. Then, at the end of this week of labor, God creates Adam. Adam's lifeless body stands before God, who then *breathes* life into the world's first man. Adam's eyes open. The first thing he sees is Yahweh Himself. And what does God do? He adores him. He blesses him. He embraces him. He *loves* him. Then He takes the rest of the week off to spend time with His newborn son, Adam.

Only now do we realize that those first days of creation, the invention of water and gravity and molecules and forests and DNA and everything else, were nothing else than the modern-day equivalent of an expecting father painting the spare bedroom in anticipation of his firstborn son. Parents today build cribs; God invented grass. We buy strollers; God formed rivers. We pick out teddy bears; God made actual bears. Can you see that we aren't the seal of creation? We are the motivation for creation. God made it all for us!

> *"And God said, 'See I have given you every herb that yields seed which is on the face of all the earth, and every tree whose fruit yields seed; to you it shall be for food.'" (Genesis 1:29)*

That's what the word "subdue" means. That's why He gave us "dominion." It was designed to be ours. God delighted at the thought of *your* arrival, and built a planet for *you* to enjoy. God, in every definition of the word, is your *Dad*.

Let's go back to man's first interaction with his Dad.

> "...God said to them, 'Be fruitful and multiply; fill the earth...'"

The first recorded dialogue between heavenly Father and newborn son is this: *Make more people*. What could God possibly want with more people? It'd be easy to get religious and respond with something like, "God wanted more people to accomplish His mysterious work." But what work is left at this point? Creation is complete. And the only "work" to be done is to make more people. God wasn't commanding Adam and Eve to create a team of dedicated workers, some sort of heavenly assembly-line to manufacture songs for Christian radio stations. He was commissioning them to expand God's family, to bring more souls into this world who could be the recipients of the Almighty's love.

It's amazing how much of this we've missed. After all, John did tell us that "God is love" (1 John 4:8). Why would we expect anything less from God?

Unfortunately, Adam and Eve's story ends with their fall, and century after century passes by with each generation walking further and further away from God. But then Noah found favor in God's eyes.

> "So God blessed Noah and his sons, and said to them: 'Be fruitful and multiply, and fill the earth.'" (Genesis 9:1)

It's the same command: *bring people back to me. I still love you guys*.

Several chapters and several years pass, and Abram enters the scene.

> "Now the Lord had said to Abram: 'Get out of your country, from your family and from your father's house, to a land that I

> *will show you. I will make you a great nation; I will bless you and make your name great; and you shall be a blessing.'"*
> *(Genesis 12:1-2)*

God expounds upon His promise three chapters later:

> *"Then He brought [Abram] outside and said, 'Look toward heaven, and count the stars if you are able to number them.' And He said to him, 'So shall your descendants be.'" (Genesis 15:5)*

Maybe that is why God stuck a billion glow-in-the-dark stars on the ceiling of Adam's bedroom. *This is how big I want My family to be, son. This is how much love I am capable of.*

God offered the same relationship to Abraham's son, Isaac, too:

> *"'Dwell in this land, and I will be with you and bless you...'" (Genesis 26:3)*

Isaac grew up, got married, and had kids of his own. And as expected, God revealed Himself to Isaac's progeny as well:

> *"And behold, the Lord stood above [the ladder] and said: 'I am the Lord God of Abraham your father and the God of Isaac; the land on which you lie I will give to you and your descendants. Also your descendants shall be as the dust of the earth; you shall spread abroad to the west and the east, to the north and the south; and in you and in your seed all the families of the earth shall be blessed. Behold, I am with you and will keep you wherever you go, and will bring you back to this land; for I will not leave you until I have done what I have spoken to you.'" (Genesis 28:13-15)*

Can you feel God's affection, His adoration, His unequivocal love for His kids? Is the big picture coming together? God wants to know you. God wants to father you. God wants to be with you.

He promised the same thing to Moses, over and over and over again.

"I will be your God, and you will be My people."

He said it to Joshua, to David, to anyone who would listen.

"I will never leave you. I am with you."

These themes abound throughout the entire bible, both new and old testaments.

"I will take care of you."

A Proper View of Love

Yet somehow, the church has allowed religious tradition to strip God's love of its meaning. All Christians profess that God does, in fact, love them, but many aren't confident that He actually *likes* them. We often differentiate these terms when attempting the long and arduous journey of Walking in Love.

"Oh, Jeff?" you'll say. "Yeah, I *love* him… I just don't *like* him." And whenever someone says this, they stretch out the word "love" to emphasize the fact that they don't actually love Jeff, even though they know they are mandated to. Despite the Beloved Apostle's warning in 1 John 3:18, we somehow think that we can simply claim love without any corresponding action whatsoever. As if invoking the word "love" will negate every attitude, action, and behavior we live by.

A lot of people view God's love in the same exact way. "Sure, God loves me," they confess, but quickly clarify, "because He has to." What a lie from the pit of hell! This attitude stems from the sense of unworthiness the church has been laying upon its parishioners for millennia, and we will address that later, but for now, simply look at the way that God has spoken to His beloved family thus far. *"I will bless you… I will be with you… I will give to you… I am with you… I am your God… wherever you go."*

God never actually mutters the word "love" in *any* of these interactions recorded in the book of Genesis. It's all implied through His actions. He does say that He wants to be close to you. He does say that He wants to take care of you. He does say that He will never leave you. But we see His *love* through His actions. The fact that He even *wants* to be near us. The fact that He adores us. God hasn't promised to love you from a distance. Instead, He desires to be close to us, to be near to His beloved people. God desires an up-close, personal, intimate relationship with you.

What God Really Thinks of You

Let's observe this from a slightly different angle. So far, we've seen that God created the world for you, that He desires to be near to you, that He simply adores you. He promised to bless you, He said He'd never leave you, that He will always stick with you. So let me ask you this: *What does that say about you?* Think of it. God, the Creator of the universe, the King of kings and Lord of lords, Jehovah-Shalom and -Shammah and a dozen other fancy names, wants to have a relationship with Y-O-U. Correct me if I'm wrong, but you must be an alright guy (or gal).

I remember when I was a senior in high school, I met Ashton Kutcher. I had gone to a live taping of "That 70s Show" in Studio City, and afterwards, while the security guards had their backs turned, I snuck stealthily through the railing and onto the set, where I ate birthday cake with the cast, downed a few root beers with the crew, and put Demi Moore to flight by requesting an autograph. I tried to chat with one actor who will go unnamed, but he was pretty rude, so I set my sights on Ashton.

He was actually quite friendly. He signed a few autographs, posed for a couple of pictures, and before I knew it, I found myself in the midst of a conversation about the merits of Kabala. However, I had a curfew to catch, so I politely dismissed myself, took some cake for the road, and made the long drive back home, where I promptly uploaded the evidence of my Hollywood encounter onto my Myspace account.

I have to confess: I thought I was pretty cool. Looking back, it's entirely stupid (and entirely embarrassing to admit). I mean, Ashton Kutcher is just a guy. Nothing against him personally. He was a nice guy, but he was still simply *just a guy*. Yet meeting him made me feel pretty cool. *He didn't even know my name!* But being a wayward seventeen year old, I thought I was pretty sly, pretty awesome, pretty important.

How much more should we feel this way in the presence of our God? Not only have we been afforded the opportunity to meet *God*, but God actually likes us, pursues us, wants a relationship with us. Heck, He even knows your name! He knew it before you knew it. On the scale of importance, your life must be *very important* if God Himself shows an interest in you. Maybe you aren't as worthless as you think.

I know that for some of you reading this, you might be wondering why I'm spending so much time hammering in the fact that "God actually loves you." Quite simply, *because it's super important to know!* How can anyone expect to cultivate an intimate relationship with God when they don't even believe that God is interested in pursuing the relationship? How can you expect God to show you who He has made you to be, when you think you're as valuable as dirt? You need to believe that you are someone God actually wants to know. God didn't *end up with you*. For thousands of years, He's been waiting for you!

You are called to mighty things. You are. That is just a fact. But the things, the calling, the destiny, all of that stuff, is secondary to *you*. When you accepted Jesus as the Lord of your life, a transformation took place. You changed. We will discuss that in a couple chapters, but before we travel any further, it is imperative that we discuss something a little more important than us. And that, my friend, is God.

Final Thoughts

What an exciting thing it is to come to the realization that God actually *wants* to know you! If you're reading this and cannot say that you've ever accepted God's offer to become a part of His family, then it is incredibly important that you accept that invitation right now. This entire book is contingent on whether or not you have allowed God access into your life. The eponymous "Unfair Advantage," the intimate friendship with God, and heaven itself cannot be yours unless you decide to join God's family, which is only possible due to Jesus' death and resurrection. If you would like to become God's son or daughter, say this prayer now:

God, I want to be a part of Your family. I want to know You. I'm sorry that I ignored you before, but I need You to be a part of my life. I believe that Jesus died for my sins, but also that You raised Him back to life. I, too, need to be raised to life. Come into my life, Jesus, and be my King. Change me, so that I'm more like you. I love you! Amen!

Wow. Easy, huh? If that was the first time you've ever said that, then welcome to God's family. Now we can move onto the next chapter.

Small Group Questions

1. How does this chapter relate to what you're currently reading in the bible?

2. Why did God create people?

3. Why did God create you?

4. Why did God create the earth?

5. What is man's commission on the earth?

6. What are some actions that demonstrate God's love for you? Come up with at least one from the bible and one from your own life.

7. Read Genesis 1:28-29. What is one notable thing about this verse?

8. What was the main point of this chapter?

2
World's Best Dad

I remember a specific evening at a friend's house so vividly. Several years ago, my friend Robert invited my wife Cheyne and me over for dinner with his family. Those present included his wife Lori, his seven-year-old son Josh, and Cheyne and me.

Dinner was delicious! Marinated steak grilled to perfection, buttery barbeque asparagus, cheesy mashed potatoes, and Robert's special lemonade, which upon inquiry, we discovered was two-thirds sprite and one-third sweet'n sour.

After our scrumptious meal we retired to the living room, where we started watching a movie. Of course, if you're blessed enough to be married, you know that "watching a movie" really means "straining with all your effort to hear what the actors are actually saying while the women irreverently chat and ask obvious questions, seemingly unaware that a movie screening is taking place." The men strained, the women chatted, Brad Pitt acted, and key scenes were rewound and re-watched to none effect as the evening steadily continued.

About half way through the flick, Josh ran into the room, eyes ablaze. "Daddy, daddy! What's electricity?" he questioned. It was refreshing to see a young boy eagerly attempting to quench the insatiable hunger of his expanding mind.

As a young college student, I felt it was my responsibility (and their privilege) to offer a scientific explanation, so I threw myself into the midst of their conversation and began to use words like "electrons" and "charge." But before I could launch very deep into my dissertation, Robert interrupted me.

"I've got this, Garrett." And turning to Josh, "Well, son, I could *tell* you how electricity works," he lovingly said, "but wouldn't it be more fun if I *showed* you how it works?"

"Yes!" Josh squealed with delight. "That would be *so* awesome!" His excitement was tangible.

Robert stood to his feet and walked towards the kitchen, Josh nipping at his heels. I stood up and followed, slightly embarrassed at his gentle rebuke but still looking forward to the experiment that lay ahead. Would he slip his shoes off, drag his socks across the carpet, and shock a doorknob? Maybe something with a potato and a light bulb? Who knows, he could even tie a kite to a key, throw on some knickerbockers, and head out into a storm. The possibilities were endless.

Once in the kitchen, Robert opened the center drawer next to the stove, reached in, and produced a metallic fork. "Son, here's what you're going to do," he instructed. "This is a fork. I want you to go into your room and unplug your cell phone charger from the outlet." I chuckled at the notion of a seven year old having a cell phone. "After that, I want you to take this fork and shove it into the outlet. Then you will know what electricity is."

Josh's face lit up, full of wonder, and he took to the hallway towards his room. Robert stood up and quite normally returned to the living room, where he sat down in "his spot" next to his wife. She leaned over, softly kissing him as she whispered, "You're such a great dad." He picked up the remote control, aimed it at the TV, pressed "play," and "The Curious Case of Benjamin Button" resumed.

The movie was interrupted several seconds later, when all of the lights in the house flickered on and off a couple times. The television shut off, and Benjamin Button was no more. "So much for the movie," Robert said playfully, and we all laughed and laughed.

And that was the night I learned how to be a great father.

Our Dad in Heaven

I hope it's obvious that this story isn't true. In fact, it's the opposite of true. It's false. I completely made it up. I consider this story a modern-day parable, and it serves to illustrate how completely ludicrous our view of our heavenly Father can be.

In reality, Robert is a great father. He actually has two kids now, and they are both quite fantastic. His entire family is heavily involved in the church and in the community, and they truly love the Lord. I can list many reasons why Robert is a great dad, but Number One on the list is this: *He wouldn't tell his kid to stick a fork in an outlet.* If Robert would suggest, let alone allow his son to do something so self-destructive, he would automatically be disqualified from *ever* receiving a "World's Best Dad" mug for his birthday. He'd also probably have his kids taken away from him. He'd also probably be put in prison. He'd also probably be labeled "mentally unstable." Needless to say, he wouldn't be speaking at a Parenting Conference any time soon.

When we consider this parable, it's blatantly clear that this is not good parenting. So my question is this: Why don't we examine God's parenting skills by the same criteria?

Jesus, instructing His followers concerning the character and nature of God, made this statement:

> *"'If you then, being evil, know how to give good gifts to your children, how much more will your Father who is in heaven give good things to those who ask Him!'" (Matthew 7:11)*

Jesus claims that God's parenting skills make the best parent on the planet look "evil." What a tremendous statement! What tremendous faith in God's goodness! Had Jesus preached the Sermon on the Mount today, the verse would have read,

> *"'God is such a good Dad, He makes Atticus Finch look like Al Bundy.'"*

God is a great Dad. I'll say it again. God is a great Dad! I want you to notice that I used the word "Dad," not "Father." This was intentional. The reason is because when most words enter into the "Christianese" vernacular, this signifies that the church has most likely warped its meaning. The English word "Father" is defined as "a man who exercises paternal care over other persons; paternal protector or provider," but when the church uses it, that's not what it means.

Listen to the average prayer of your typical youth group volunteer. "Father God, we just pray that you would help us, Lord God, that you would just move in this place, Lord Father God, and Lord Father, Father God, if it's Your will, Father God Lord, help Susie, Lord God Father," and so on. "Father" has become the Christianese version of "um" and "like." It's a placeholder to us, not a relationship.

"Father" isn't even a word we use nowadays. The only times I think I ever used that word was when I was in *really* big trouble with my dad (a few steps beyond "suspended from school" trouble), and when giving a presentation on George Washington. It is a distant word. It doesn't typify closeness. It doesn't exemplify love. It says that God is either incredibly mad at you, or that He is incredibly far away.

Try calling God your "Dad" in your private prayer times. It'll definitely feel awkward at first, but once you overcome the embarrassment (isn't it funny how easy it is to get embarrassed during private prayer?), watch what it will do to your relationship with God. It'll bring Him close to you; more accurately, it'll bring you close to Him. You'll begin to see that God is indeed your Dad, that He loves you and protects you and desires to father you.

Then, if you want to raise a few eyebrows, refer to God as your Dad during group prayer. Man oh man, that'll make some people uncomfortable! They usually get a little confused at first, thinking your earth-dad just walked in and interrupted the prayer meeting. Then, one by one, it'll dawn on them that you're just having a conversation with your Dad. Some will welcome the new designation. Others will overthink it. A few will wonder why *they* never thought of it. They *all* will try it at home that night. And over the course of a few weeks, every last one of them will begin to experience a closer, more intimate relationship with their Heavenly Dad. A relational revolution will have begun.

World's Best Dad

If there is one thing that Christians love to do, it's to blame God for things He didn't do.

It's actually something the church excels at. Take any sickness, any tragic event, any natural disaster... somehow, God is behind it. It might be the kid behind you in geometry who has the sniffles: "Yeah, it sucks. But God must be trying to teach me something." It could be a coworker whose cousin died prematurely: "I just don't get it. Kim was such a sweet girl. But you know, God works in mysterious ways." Whatever ailment befalls us, we are always able to somehow skew it into something that it's not: a "blessing" from God.

But one has to wonder: why would we allow God to get away with things that we wouldn't excuse the worst parents from? If a student has bruises he received from his father, who was "teaching him a lesson," the teacher would be expected to call Child Protective Services. But if a child shows up to church in a cast because God was "teaching him a lesson," the Sunday School teacher is expected to praise God? Does this double standard make any sense whatsoever?

Jesus taught that God was the best Dad we could possibly imagine. He's not Homer Simpson. We might expect Peter Griffin to be abusive (though we still wouldn't excuse it), but we'd expect a lot more from wise TV dad Mr. Cleaver. Yet for some illogical reason, we excuse God from actions that'd be unacceptable for even an alcoholic father. Why is that?

One word: *omniscience*. In other words, God is smarter than us. And since God is smarter than us, we find it acceptable to blame Him for things that make absolutely no sense. We chalk it off to His "mysterious ways," His "divine plan," as if that somehow makes it good.

As with most words inducted into the Christianese Dictionary, we've had to redefine "good" to make it consistent with our tainted view of God. Whereas the normal definition of "good" is *morally excellent, virtuous, righteous, proper,* and *well-behaved,* we've translated it as

> Good. (Adjective) Bad plus omniscient.

And if asked to use it in a sentence, we'd offer something to the effect of:

> *God gave my sister a terminal illness, but He's still good. Praise Him!*

How could we have been so deceived? For centuries, we've looked at the horrors of history, from the bubonic plague to tsunamis to AIDS, and attributed these horrendous things to God. Car accidents: God. Death in the family: God. Skiing accident: God. And yet when something good comes around, like a promotion at work or an "A" on a math test, God is the last person we want to give credit to.

God is not responsible for the pain in your life. God is not a harbinger of death. God is good. *God is good.* Not Christianese *good.* Not "actually bad but let's call it *good."* He is really good.

Look at what the scriptures say.

> *"Every good gift and every perfect gift is from above, and comes down from the Father of lights, with whom there is no variation or shadow of turning." (James 1:17)*

I like how simply the New Living Translation says it: *"Whatever is good and perfect comes down to us from God our Father."*

I don't know if you can get any clearer than that. *God is good. Everything good comes from God.* James takes it a step further, saying that the things God brings into our lives are *perfect*. If there is something in your life that cannot be aptly described as either *good* or *perfect*, then you don't have the right to name God as its source. And James tops it all off by claiming that the reason God brings us *good* and *perfect* things is simply because He is our Father. He's your Abba Daddy. And just as James said, just as Jesus said, He desires to give you good things.

So then, where do *bad* things come from? The cold that your brother is battling? The arthritis that has crippled your grandmother? Hurricane Sandy? If they don't come from your Dad, what is their source?

> *"'The thief does not come except to steal, and to kill, and to destroy...'" (John 10:10)*

What a second. You're telling me that *the devil* is the bad guy? I almost have to laugh at how blind the church has been. Of course the devil is the bad guy! That's kind of *his* thing. Jesus is pretty straightforward about the devil's handiwork. Stealing. Killing. Destroying. That's what he does. Cancer steals life, kills people, and destroys families. Therefore, it cannot be from God. This single scripture will clarify a century of bad doctrine, if you will accept it.

The Abundant Life

We can plainly see that it is the devil that is behind all thievery, death, and destruction in your life. "But God allows it," some of you might say. "God may not *cause*" (and they always emphasize the word *cause*) "the pain in your life, but He certainly *allows* it." Ignoring the fact that we are now making your loving Dad a co-conspirator with the devil, let's allow the scriptures to bring light into this discussion.

> *"'The thief does not come except to steal, and to kill, and to destroy. I have come that they may have life...'" (John 10:10)*

Jesus identifies His purpose on earth as bringing *life* to combat the evils of the devil. Notice what Jesus *did not* say:

> *"The thief does not come except to steal, and to kill, and to destroy. I have come to help you put up with it."*

Or maybe something like this:

> *"I have come to give you inner peace in the midst of your trial."*

Nope. That's not what it says. Jesus came to bring *life*. Life! The opposite of death! The opposite of sickness! The opposite of everything the devil holds dear! Jesus brings *life* to those who welcome it. And not *just* life.

> *"...I have come that they may have life, and that they may have it more abundantly."* (John 10:10)

You were created to live an *abundant life*! It's what Jesus said! Quickly referencing a concordance, we will find that the word "abundantly" (the Greek *perissos*) is quite a loaded word. It carries with it these meanings:
- *Over and above, more than is necessary, superadded*
- *Exceedingly abundantly, supremely*
- *Superior, extraordinary, surpassing, uncommon*
- *Advantage, more eminent, more remarkable, more excellent*

Your Dad doesn't just combat the devil; He *creams* him! He goes out of His way to bless you "exceedingly abundantly" at the devil's expense. He opposes satan's work, and then adds some more blessings on top, just in case you still weren't sure. This is your Dad!

I hope the point is clear: *God is a good Dad*! He isn't out to "get" you. It's incredibly silly to say things like "God must be trying to teach me something" whenever something bad happens to you. Think about it: God is *trying* to get some abstract point across to you, and has no better method of communication than an ambiguous cold with some esoteric meaning? I thought God was omniscient. And in His infinite wisdom, influenza is His preferred messenger? A broken arm is God's equivalent to an email?

Search the scriptures for *one* example of God communicating to a Christian through sickness, pain, or suffering. You won't find any. Not one. Believe me, I've looked. And I've never met someone who could find one, either. What you do find is God speaking to His people in other, more practical ways.

> *"As they ministered to the Lord and fasted, the Holy Spirit <u>said</u>, 'Now separate to Me Barnabas and Saul for the work to which I have called them.'" (Acts 13:2)*

Hold the phone. The Holy Spirit *said*? Surely this is a misprint. I thought that God communicated to us through random events and undecipherable circumstances. But maybe, just maybe, we were wrong. Maybe God *doesn't* use circumstances to get His points across.

Often, Christians try to make things too spiritual. If a Christian falls off a ladder and needs to be rushed to the ER, he might wonder to himself, "I bet God wants me to witness to someone at the hospital." That's what you deciphered from your eight-foot plummet off the roof? The bump on your head must be worse than we thought! I'd love to hear how that attempt at witnessing would transpire.

"Hi, my name is Garrett. God shoved me off a ladder this afternoon. Do you want to know why? He's got His eyes on you!"

It sounds more like a warning than a sermon. "God pushed me off a ladder, and you're next! Run!" It's completely ridiculous! If God wanted you to go to the hospital, He would tell you the same way He told Paul and Barnabas. He'd *say* it. It's a lot easier than resorting to violence.

Another phrase the church has coined over the years is that "God works in mysterious ways." However, it's never used in a good context, like "I thought my rent was going to be late, but someone paid it for me! God works in mysterious ways!" No, it's always more grim, like "I can't believe my younger sister is in the hospital again! But we know God has a purpose behind this. After all, He does work in mysterious ways!"

I found this view so revolting that I decided to study it out. I searched out the word "mystery" in the bible to determine whether or not God *actually* works in mysterious ways (it's good to base your views of God on the bible; after all, He wrote it). What I found was shocking. Of the twenty-seven times the word "mystery" (the Greek *mysterion*) appears in the bible, twenty-six of them *specifically* say that the "mystery" has already been revealed to the church through scripture. There is only one time that the "mystery" is not revealed to the church:

> *"For he who speaks in a tongue does not speak to men but to God, for no one understands him; however, in the spirit he speaks mysteries." (1 Corinthians 14:2)*

Do you see it yet? God isn't some distant enigma we can never hope to understand. I once heard a pastor claim that "a human who can understand what God is doing is like an ant that can understand a computer." That pastor was wrong! God wants to be understood. He went out of His way to *reveal* the mystery to us, to make it crystal clear. And if anyone is capable of establishing valid lines of communication with the human race, it's omniscient God. He doesn't need circumstance, weather, pain, destruction, or the devil to get a point across.

> *"Then [God] said, 'Go out, and stand on the mountain before the Lord.' And behold, the Lord passed by, and a great and strong wind tore into the mountains and broke the rocks in pieces before the Lord, but the Lord was not in the wind; and after the wind an earthquake, but the Lord was not in the earthquake; and after the earthquake a fire, but the Lord was not in the fire; and after the fire a still small voice." (1 Kings*

19:11-12)

Notice how God *didn't* speak to Elijah. It wasn't through the wind. It wasn't through the earthquake. It wasn't through the fire. The scriptures go out of their way to tell you how God *doesn't* speak. It's not through weather. It's not through destruction. It's not through some spectacular show. If that was how God spoke to His people, we'd need a translation book to decode the meanings. In fact, there actually are plenty of ludicrous books written for this very purpose. Ministries have released books that will supposedly tell you what God is trying to speak through your cancer. A sore left shoulder is different than a sore right shoulder. It's completely insane. But the bible teaches us that God speaks in a very straightforward way: He speaks. That is how God speaks. By speaking. It's pretty simple when you think about it.

I think it's important to be very specific here. There are *two* ways that God will communicate to you. The first is through His Word. The second is through the Holy Spirit. And if you ever believe that the Holy Spirit has spoken something to you that is contrary to His Word, then it's not the Holy Spirit speaking. But this chapter is not intended to teach you how God speaks. Its purpose is to demonstrate that God is a good Dad, one who doesn't need to resort to obscure circumstances, "mysterious ways," and ultimately child abuse to relate to you.

God is good. *God is good.* Whenever I worship God, I always find myself saying this to Him over and over again. *You are good.* It's such a simple thing to say. *You are so good.* Yet so many Christians who profess it don't actually believe it. Sure, they say it, but they don't expect it. *Dad, you are so incredibly good.*

Final Thoughts

I had a preplanned way I intended to end this chapter. It was pretty clever (if I do say so myself), and tied into the next chapter nicely, but God is taking us in a different direction.

Pray this right now. Wherever you are, say these words to your Dad. If you're in public, politely dismiss yourself and draw near to your heavenly Father.

Dad, I love You so much! Thank You for being so good to me. I'm sorry I've blamed You for things You didn't do. I know the truth now. You are absolutely good! Thank You for loving me. Thank You for taking care of me. Thank You for always being with me.

I want to know You as my Dad. I want that close Father-Son relationship that Jesus said I could have with You. I invite You into every part of my life. I give You permission to father me. Teach me how to be more like You. Teach me how to grow up into the man (or woman) of God that You want me to be. Raise me up to be more like You, to be more like my Dad. I love You so much. In Jesus' precious name, Amen.

Small Group Questions

1. How does this chapter relate to what you're currently reading in the bible?

2. Consider the best father you know, either real or fictitious. How do they stack up to God the Father?

3. Why do you think Christians attribute evil things to God?

4. Can you think of a single biblical example of God bringing harm to a Christian?

5. When loved ones pass away, people often make statements like, "God took her from us before it was her time." In light of the scriptures, is that statement true?

6. According to the bible, how does God communicate with Christians?

7. Read Matthew 7:9-11. What is one notable thing about this verse?

8. What was the main point of this chapter?

3
Why Do You Call Me Good?

"Why *did* he call Me good?"

Have you ever been reading your bible, then without realizing it you suddenly switch over to auto-pilot? Some distraction pops into your head... maybe you're wondering what's for dinner, maybe you're expecting a text message from a friend, maybe you're (once again) pondering who would win in a fight between Wolverine and the Terminator... and you sort of zone out. Your eyes are still reading the scriptures, but you aren't processing any of it. Then all of a sudden, you realize that it's been five minutes, you've read three chapters, and you remember *none* of it?

Don't feel guilty. This happens to me too. More than I'd like to admit. It's not that you find that particular portion of the bible boring; it's just that you've read it before. Your mind recognizes that it is familiar with that biblical passage, so it begins to wander.

Well, this happened to me once when I was reading through the Gospel of Matthew. I was reading through the story of the Rich Young Ruler and had slipped into mindless skimming when Jesus snapped me out of it.

"Why did he call Me good?" He asked me.

If you read through the life of Jesus, you'll find that He often asked questions to elicit wisdom. He'd question His disciples: "Who do *you* say that I am?" He'd question His adversaries: "John's baptism, is it from God or man?" He'd question the multitudes: "What did you come out to see?" I've learned during my brief time on this earth that when Jesus asks a question, it's because the answer is incredibly important.

"Why did he call Me good?"

I knew Jesus was trying to teach me something, so I flipped back a few verses to read the passage in context.

> *"Now behold, one came and said to Jesus, 'Good Teacher, what good thing shall I do that I may have eternal life?' So He said to him, 'Why do you call Me good?'" (Matthew 19:16-17)*

Jesus asked me again, "Why did he call Me good?" In the years I had spent studying the bible, I had never thought to answer that question. I mean, I knew that Jesus *was* good. I had never thought to ask *why* a first-century Jew would think so. But apparently, it was an important enough question that Jesus felt compelled to ask it back then and repeat it to me two thousand years later.

I scanned the scripture again. "Why did he call Jesus good?" I asked myself. Then I noticed something peculiar. The rich young ruler used the word "good" twice in that verse.

"'<u>Good</u> Teacher, what <u>good</u> thing shall I do...?'"

In an instant, I realized the answer to Jesus' question. *The young man believed Jesus was good because Jesus did good things*! This shouldn't come as a shock to us. After all, most of the world functions under this assumption.

Consider most of the world religions that exist today. Muslims *must* obey the Five Pillars of Islam to be right with Allah. According to the Qur'an, Muslims are required to profess Islam, pray five times a day in the direction of Mecca, give 2.5% of their wealth to the needy, fast during Ramadan, and make a *hajj* (or pilgrimage) to Mecca during their lifetime. Without performing these five essential duties, they *cannot* be right with Allah, and will not enter into paradise.

Buddhists also have a list of rules that must be met in order to achieve nirvana. They have their Four Noble Truths:

> *Noble Truth 1*: Life sucks.
> *Noble Truth 2*: Life sucks because you want things.
> *Noble Truth 3*: Embrace Life Sucking, and it will no longer matter that life sucks.
> *Noble Truth 4*: You embrace Life Sucking through the Eightfold Path, and thus achieve Nirvana.

It is through strict adherence to these four noble truths and the eightfold path that one can hope to enter into nirvana, or the eternal bliss of the afterlife.

Even the Jews have distorted the intention of the Mosaic Law to create a system of works. Moses gave Israel 613 laws (called *Mitzvah*) to show them their utter depravity, but they believed that through obedience to those rules they could become good. For some reason, the ancient rabbis of old thought that 613 rules wasn't enough, so they expanded it with a document called the *Talmud*, which was over six thousand pages long and added thousands of additional rules into the mix.

Every one of these religions believes that humans are responsible for their own salvation. Even the world religions that have long since faded into history cherished this view. The Greeks and Romans saw their deities as selfish, prideful, arrogant, mean-spirited, unstable, and all around human, and believed that it was through man's own innate goodness that they could survive the wrath of the gods.

And have you ever wondered why Madonna and Angelina Jolie keep adopting babies? Why celebrities incessantly get involved in politics and other such things they know nothing about? Why entrepreneurs and politicians hold galas and fundraisers and donate billions to charity? These things, these *actions*, don't come out of the goodness of their hearts. On the contrary, they come from the depravity of their hearts. Just like people all around the world, they have come to the alarming realization that *they are not good people*.

The human race is not *good*; it is inherently *sinful*. Remember back to when you were young. Your parents had to teach you such profound lessons as "be nice to others" and "do the right thing." Why? Why was it necessary to spend eighteen years training you to behave yourself? Because it was *unnatural*! The human race is naturally greedy, rude, proud, and mean. It is *sinful*. This is a fundamental truth that every human on earth is aware of, whether they will admit it or not: *we are born with an inherent sinful nature.*

The Fall of Man

Of course, we can trace this sinful nature back to Eden. Eve is out on an afternoon stroll through the garden while her man is at home, probably watching the big game (the bears versus the eagles), when she is approached by that cunning serpent of old. He goads her into breaking God's one rule, saying,

> *"'God knows that in the day you eat of it your eyes will be opened, and you will be like God, knowing good and evil.'" (Genesis 3:5)*

Here is my question: weren't Adam and Eve *already* like God?

> *"Then God said, 'Let Us make man in Our image, according to Our likeness…'" (Genesis 1:26)*

I want you to see this. Adam and Eve were built to be *just like God*. That was God's original intention for you. Some people are reading this right now, thinking to themselves, "Yeah, but that's not what that verse means," so before we let the religious fog sweep in and blind us from this truth, let's look at another scripture to gain context of what it means to be "in someone's image and likeness."

> *"And Adam lived one hundred and thirty years, and begot a son <u>in his own likeness</u>, <u>after his image</u>, and named him Seth." (Genesis 5:3)*

This is the only other time in the entire bible that these two phrases are used together, and it compares the similarities between a father and his son. *We were designed to be God's children.* We were designed to look like Him, talk like Him, act like Him, *be like Him*. Before we return to our discussion on the sinful nature of man, just dwell on this truth for a few moments. *You were meant to be like God.* While the Greeks created their gods in their own image, showcasing the evil traits of mankind, God made you in His image, with the intent of showcasing His perfect qualities. *You were meant to be like Him.* Let that sink in.

However, as discussed before, the human race did fall. It's precisely what God had warned would happen.

> *"And the Lord God commanded the man, saying, 'Of every tree of the garden you may freely eat; but of the tree of the knowledge of good and evil you shall not eat, for in the day that you eat of it you shall surely die.'" (Genesis 2:16-17)*

Now, we know that Adam didn't die *physically* that day. He went on to live to the ripe old age of nine hundred and thirty. God wasn't warning Adam of physical death. It was *spiritual death* that He was concerned about. Adam was a spirit being, just like his Dad (John 4:24), but dying spiritually caused Adam to *no longer be like God*. All the evils of this world, all the problems with the human race, everything that is wrong with society can be traced back to this pivotal moment. *You shall surely die.*

When read in the original Hebrew language, this literally reads *"dying you shall die."* God warned Adam, "If you break this one rule, you will die spiritually, and spiritual death will bring death into every part of your life." Physical death is a result of spiritual death. Sickness is a result of spiritual death. Poverty, unhappiness, everything that is wrong in the world, has grown out of the spiritual death that has plagued mankind for ages. And this spiritual death that consumed the human race on that fateful day is called the *"sinful nature."*

It'd be really easy to stop the book right here. In fact, most Christians believe this is where the story ends. "Man is a fallen creature, contaminated with a sinful nature, but God loves us *in spite of our sin*. The end." But listen, this is not the end of our story. No, this is just the beginning. Things are about to get really good.

One Way to the Top

As I said before, mankind has tried in vain for thousands of years to earn salvation on our own. I think the best example of this is found at the Tower of Babel. God had recently commanded the human race to "fill the earth," so of course the humans, under the leadership of a guy named Nimrod (who lives up to his namesake), decided to do the exact opposite.

> *"And they said, 'Come, let us build ourselves a city, and a tower whose top is in the heavens; let us make a name for ourselves, lest we be scattered abroad over the face of the whole earth.'" (Genesis 11:4)*

They had the brilliant idea that if they worked hard enough, they could secure their own salvation. And this has been the pattern of humanity since Adam's fall. So much so that this worldview is actually called "humanism." According to the World English Dictionary, "humanism" is defined as

> *"The rejection of religion in favor of a belief in the advancement of humanity by its own efforts."*

It's what atheists believe. It's what the Greeks and Romans believed. It's what Buddhists believe. It's what Muslims believe. It's what Orthodox Jews believe. It's what most philanthropists and politicians and celebrities and teachers believe. It's the basic worldview of every society, and every single religion and philosophy and –ism believes it. With the exception of one.

The entire world will insist that if you do good things, that will make you a good person. That's why community service is considered punishment. "You broke the rules, so we'll cancel out your transgression with a few good deeds." When I was ten, I was arrested for breaking into an ore refinery and playing with their walkie talkies. The judge sentenced me to eighty hours of community service, which I served out by playing Bingo with senior citizens. But playing Bingo didn't flow out of the goodness of my heart. I actually *hated* it. Eighty hours of serving others didn't make me any better than I had been before. The world's system of salvation had failed me.

"*Doing good things will make you a good person.*" That's what the rich young ruler thought. That's why he came to Jesus for salvation.

"Jesus, you're a good person. You must be, because you've done so many good things. What good things can I do so that I, too, may be considered a good person?"

Jesus shoots him out of the water.

> "*So He said to him, 'Why do you call Me good? No one is good but One, that is, God.'" (Matthew 19:17)*

This statement used to throw me because it almost sounds like Jesus is saying that He *isn't* good. "*Why are you calling Me good, because I'm not*" seems to be the implication. "*No one is good but God.*" What is Jesus trying to teach us here? He is forcing the rich young ruler to consider the source of Jesus' goodness. Is Jesus good because He does good things, or is He good because that is His nature? Jesus gives us a huge hint by pointing away from works and towards His Dad. *Only God can make someone good.*

While the rest of the world is running around in circles, maintaining that doing good things will make you a good person, Christianity stands in stark contrast. That is what makes the Christian religion so unique. It is the only belief system in the universe to ever claim that we *cannot do it on our own*. We can't make ourselves good; we can only *be made* good by One, that is, God.

That was the whole purpose of the Old Testament law. Today, Christians are fighting over the law. Some say the law is horrible and evil and bad, while the other faction of believers claims that the law is tremendously good and that we all need to live under its tutelage. I hate to break it to you, but both groups are wrong.

> *"Is the law then against the promises of God? Certainly not! For if there had been a law given which could have given life, truly righteousness would have been by the law. But the Scripture has confined all under sin, that the promise by faith in Jesus Christ might be given to those who believe. But before faith came, we were kept under guard by the law, kept for the faith which would afterward be revealed. Therefore the law was our tutor to bring us to Christ, that we might be justified by faith. But after faith has come, we no longer are under a tutor. For you are all sons of God through faith in Christ Jesus." (Galatians 3:21-26)*

The Law of Moses was never meant to make us righteous. It was never meant to make us good. It was meant to show us that no matter how hard we tried, we couldn't make ourselves good. We could never live up to God's standard. We could never bring ourselves back to life. Those 613 mitzvahs given on Mount Sinai were simply meant to put our sinful nature under the microscope, so that it'd be blatantly clear that we were broken.

But it was more than that. It wasn't just another way for God to show us we were screw-ups. He wasn't just rubbing it in our faces that we were totally depraved. Yes, He wanted us to know we were inherently sinful, but only so we would know to look for help. The Law was a giant red arrow, a heavenly GPS of sorts, pointing directly towards the Great Physician, the only One who could cure us of our infection. The Law was God's way of bringing us to Christ.

And what happened once we came to Christ in faith? Did God pat us on the back, and tell us it was all going to be okay? Did He look past our sinful nature, our total depravity, our spiritual

death, and say, "I still accept you"?
Actually, no. He didn't.

> *"Therefore the law was our tutor to bring us to Christ, that we might be justified by faith." (Galatians 3:24)*

The moment you came to Christ, something changed.

> *"...Justified by faith..."*

The word "justify" isn't a word we regularly use in the Western world, so let me read you its definition:
- *To render righteous*
- *To show, exhibit, and evince one to be righteous*
- *To declare and pronounce one to be just and righteous*

Like I said, when you came to Christ, something changed.

A New Heart

Salvation is another one of those words that Christians seem determined to redefine. For some, salvation means you get to go to heaven when you die. And yes, it is true that heaven is included in your salvation. But that isn't all salvation has to offer. Others will say that salvation means being delivered from the consequences of sin. That, too, is a part of salvation, but if that's all you've got, then you are barely scratching the surface. You see, salvation isn't when God looks past our sinful nature and loves us regardless. Salvation is when He removes our sinful nature and replaces it with His divine nature.

> *"'No one sews a piece of unshrunk cloth on an old garment; or else the new piece pulls away from the old, and the tear is made worse. And no one puts new wine into old wineskins; or else the new wine bursts the wineskins, the wine is spilled, and the wineskins are ruined. But new wine must be put into*

new wineskins.'" (Mark 2:21-22)

I don't know if you often wear blue jeans, but my wardrobe consists almost entirely of denim. And according to my wife, I have the innate ability to destroy a brand new pair of jeans in a matter of weeks. I don't know how it happens. I'd like to say it's the result of the epic games of kickball I play every Tuesday after work, but I'm not actually cool enough to play kickball now that I'm in my adult years. I do go on the occasional hike, but not often enough to demolish jeans at the rate I do.

Early in our marriage, we were somewhat poor, so my wife would patch up the holes in my pants to save money. Not once did she ever buy a pair of brand new jeans, cut out patches, and sew them into the old, ripped pants. That'd be crazy. For one, we couldn't afford new pants. However, if we managed to get our hands on a new pair of Levis, she wouldn't immediately destroy them. No, she'd just give me the new jeans. No need for repairs, honey, here's a new pair o' jeans.

That's the same point Jesus is making in this parable. You don't use the new (i.e., the Holy Spirit) to fix up the old (i.e., you and me). You just get rid of the old and replace it with the new. If you can afford to get something new, why keep the old? God is the same way. He doesn't leave us in our old, fallen condition. He sends the Holy Spirit, who recreates us in His own perfect image once again.

I don't know how familiar you are with wine etiquette of the first century. I'm completely unfamiliar, but apparently it was a major faux pas to put new wine into old wineskins. Jesus goes as far as saying that doing so would result in the destruction of the wineskins. This is Jesus' subtle way of informing us that we cannot handle the Holy Spirit in our degenerative state. Before we can receive the very life of God, we must be made new.

This isn't just a New Testament idea. Centuries before Jesus came on the scene, we see this same salvation described in great detail.

> *"I will give you a new heart and put a new spirit within you; I will take the heart of stone out of your flesh and give you a heart of flesh. I will put My Spirit within you and cause you to walk in My statutes, and you will keep My judgments and do them."* (Ezekiel 36:26-27)

Consider the process of salvation. First, we are given a new heart and a new spirit. Our old stony heart isn't simply mended; it's completely removed. A stony heart doesn't belong in a fleshly body. Instead, we are given a heart of flesh, the heart God intended for us to have since the beginning. Only after we've been given a new heart and a new spirit can we receive the Holy Spirit into our lives. It is these three components, the new spirit, the heart of flesh, and the Holy Spirit Himself, that are necessary for salvation, and all of these steps take place in the blink of an eye. You are new. You are good. You are alive. Salvation is complete.

Now consider the result of salvation.

> *"I will put My Spirit within you and cause you to walk in My statutes..."*

Whereas before we were indebted to a law we couldn't possibly keep, we are now naturally able to keep a law that is no longer required of us. Again, we see the fundamental difference between every man-made religion and Christianity. The world says *"doing good things will make you a good person,"* and conversely, *"doing bad things will make you a bad person."* But Jesus, as His custom was, taught a doctrine that was completely foreign to the world.

> *"'A good man out of the good treasure of his heart brings forth good things, and an evil man out of the evil treasure brings forth evil things.'"* (Matthew 12:35)

Doing good deeds doesn't make you a good person any more than barking like a dog makes you a golden retriever. It's a ludicrous notion that outward behavior could dictate inward nature. Sure, you could train a dog to walk on its hind legs and wear prescription glasses, but at the end of the day, Fido is still a dog. An entertaining dog, but a dog nonetheless. And an unredeemed man living apart from God can perform all of the good works he wants to, but ultimately, he is still an evil man who will naturally bring forth evil things.

> *"'There is nothing that enters a man from outside which can defile him; but the things which come out of him, those are the things that defile a man... for from within, out of the heart of man, proceed evil thoughts, adulteries, fornications, murders, thefts, covetousness, wickedness, deceit, lewdness, an evil eye, blasphemy, pride, foolishness. All these evil things come from within and defile a man.'" (Mark 7:15, 21-23)*

All the evils of this world come from *within* man. Jesus makes that crystal clear. It is not the outward behavior that dictates the inward nature. The issue is the heart. It's always been the heart. And as long as the heart is wicked, no amount of good behavior, community service, or charitable donations will save you. But allowing God to invade your life and make you into something new, something better... that'll take care of the heart issue once and for all.

> *"Therefore, if anyone is in Christ, he is a new creation; old things have passed away; behold, all things have become new." (2 Corinthians 5:17)*

Final Thoughts

Take a moment to examine your own life. Have you been trying to earn your own salvation? Accept the simple truth that goodness is not something to be earned, but rather something to be received. God has *already* transformed you. Don't spend your life trying to win His love. Just draw near to your loving Father.

When you have a chance, read **Galatians chapter 5**. Specifically dwell on the "Fruit of the Spirit" passage (v. 22-23). Those characteristics aren't behaviors you need to strive to live up to. The Fruit of the Spirit are the natural byproducts of a life transformed by God. If those characteristics aren't evident in your life, pray this prayer right now.

Dad, You are so incredibly good! And because I am Your child, I am good, just like You. Thank You that I am filled with the love of God that passes knowledge. Thank You that I have Your joy that no man can take. Thank You that my life is characterized by peace that passes understanding. Thank You that I am a patient person, a kind person, and a good person. Just as You are faithful, so I am faithful. Thank You that I am gentle, and that I have absolute control over myself. Thank You, Jesus, for making me just like You.

Whenever you are feeling like you aren't a loving person, or a faithful person, or a patient person, just thank your Dad that it is *already* done. God has *already* declared that these characteristics describe you, whether you can see it or not. Keep believing, and you will start to see it.

Small Group Questions

1. How does this chapter relate to what you're currently reading in the bible?

2. Why did the rich young ruler call Jesus "good"?

3. Does performing good deeds make you a good person? Does performing bad deeds make you a bad person?

4. What is the only way you can become a good person?

5. Are Christians righteous or unrighteous?

6. Why do you think it's important to distinguish that Christians are new, rather than just clean?

7. Read 2 Corinthians 5:17. What is one notable thing about this verse?

8. What was the main point of this chapter?

4

The New You

Peter Parker is bitten by a radioactive spider, but months pass before he ever dons the Spider-Man mask. Clark Kent is trained by his biological father, Jor El, in the Fortress of Solitude before he learns to fly through the skies of Metropolis. Batman spends years under the tutelage of Ra's al Ghul. Luke Skywalker's education in the ways of the Force requires completion under the guidance of Jedi Master Yoda. Professor Charles Xavier opens up a school for gifted youngsters.

These characters we adore didn't just wake up one day with superpowers and by lunchtime grow into the heroes we know and love. No, it required an understanding of who they had become before they stepped into the greatness that awaited them. After all, if no one had told Clark Kent that he was an extraterrestrial with the power of flight, do you think he'd ever have taken to the skies?

I'm reminded of the spontaneous church service Peter and John held on their way to a prayer meeting. If you'll recall, it began with a miracle.

> *"Now Peter and John went up together to the temple at the hour of prayer, the ninth hour. And a certain man lame from his mother's womb was carried, whom they had laid daily at the gate of the temple which is called Beautiful, to ask alms from those who entered the temple; who, seeing Peter and John about to go into the temple, asked for alms. And fixing his eyes on him, with John, Peter said, 'Look at us.' So he gave them his attention, expecting to receive something from them. Then Peter said, 'Silver and gold I do not have, but what I do have I give you: In the name of Jesus Christ of Nazareth, rise*

up and walk.' And he took him by the right hand and lifted him up, and immediately his feet and ankle bones received strength. So he, leaping up, stood and walked and entered the temple with them – walking, leaping, and praising God." (Acts 3:1-8)

Peter and John weren't out fishing for a supernatural encounter. They were just going to church when a guy in need came to them for help. Peter doesn't even flinch. Notice his response.

"What I do have I give you."

What was it that Peter had? What was it that triggered this healing? More importantly, *how* did Peter know? This wasn't like Clark Kent being pushed off a skyscraper, only to discover he had the power of flight. This was no accident. Peter knew something. He knew something about himself, something that had been given to him, and it sparked a revolution in Jerusalem on that fateful afternoon. So what was it that he had, and how did he discover it?

"'Behold, I give you the authority to trample on serpents and scorpions, and over all the power of the enemy, and nothing shall by any means hurt you.'" (Luke 10:19)

Peter had authority. He had power. He knew because Jesus had told him. And that knowledge was just as important as the power itself. After all, if Jesus had put the power in him secretly without telling anybody, Peter never would have had the confidence to step out and use it.

Last year, my mom gave me a treasury bond that my grandmother had purchased for me when I was five. The bond had matured when I turned fifteen, but I wasn't told about it until last September. For over ten years I had this money sitting in the bank, waiting to be used at my discretion, but because I didn't *know* about it, it was going to waste.

Sadly, this is the state of much of the church. We have been made new and we have been given tremendous power, but most Christians are completely oblivious. For two thousand years, the church has chosen to teach its faithful parishioners who we used to be rather than who we have become. As a result, we have millions upon millions of Holy Spirit power plants walking this earth, entirely unaware of the power that flows through their veins. And just like the heroes of comics and the heroes of faith mentioned above, it's time that we learned exactly who we are.

But God

Fortunately, Christians come with a detailed instruction manual, written by a fairly intelligent and omniscient Author. As Paul told his young disciple Timothy,

> *"All Scripture is given by inspiration of God, and is profitable for doctrine, for reproof, for correction, for instruction in righteousness, that the man of God may be complete, thoroughly equipped for every good work." (2 Timothy 3:16-17)*

The bible is essentially a "Christian Living for Dummies" guide, a Fortress of Solitude for the man and woman of God. Basically, it is God's way of telling you just how awesome you are. And while I am hoping that you get a ton out of this book I'm writing, it cannot compare to how much you'll get from the bible. Read your bible. Study your bible. Cherish your bible. It is God's message directly to you, and I cannot overemphasize how amazing your life will become if you'll just make God's Word the focus of your life.

One chapter in particular will be extremely helpful in uncovering who God has created you to be.

> *"And you He made alive, who were dead in trespasses and sins, in which you once walked according to the course of this*

> *world, according to the prince of the power of the air* (the devil), *the spirit who now works in the sons of disobedience, among whom also we all once conducted ourselves in the lusts of the flesh, fulfilling the desires of the flesh and of the mind, and were by nature children of wrath, just as the others."* (Ephesians 2:1-3)

Paul gives us a pretty descriptive analysis of who you used to be prior to your conversion. We know this description is past tense, because he begins it with the statement, "in which you *once* walked." This is how you used to be. You once were spiritually dead, as we uncovered in the previous chapter. As a spiritually dead individual, you lived in sin, just like the rest of the world. In fact, you lived precisely the way satan wanted you to. By your very nature, you were a sinner.

"But God."

I love that statement. You find it littered throughout the scriptures, particularly right after mankind has sunk to his lowest point.

> *"But God, who is rich in mercy, because of His great love with which He loved us, even when we were dead in trespasses, made us alive together with Christ (by grace you have been saved), and raised us up together, and made us sit together in the heavenly places in Christ Jesus."* (Ephesians 2:4-6)

I insist that you go back and read that passage at least three more times. I find it absolutely breathtaking! God doesn't just love you; He *loves* you, with an exceedingly great love. And His great love took you, you who were dead and evil and hopeless and an all-around sinner, and made you *alive*. Think of it! You became alive. Just as Adam received the breath of life ages and ages ago, and was subsequently transformed into a living being, so have you received that same breath, that same Spirit, that same *life*.

But God didn't stop there. After making you into a new being and giving you His life, He raised you up and made you to sit in the heavens. Now, I know what you're thinking. You're still here. On earth. Clearly, you're not in heaven. What is this talking about?

I'll describe it this way. As I write this, Barack Obama is currently the sitting President. Now, is he actually *sitting*? Probably not. But whether he is seated in the Oval Office or traveling the country or on vacation does not change the fact that his position is President of the United States of America. Heck, he doesn't even have to be in America to be the US President. No matter where he goes, he is still the president. And in the same way, you are officially seated in heaven despite the fact that you are physically here on planet earth.

Finally, notice how many times the word "together" is used here. "We are alive *together* with Christ… we are raised up *together* with Christ… we are sitting in heaven *together* with Christ." It seems that Jesus' motivation for coming to the earth, taking on a human body, dying on the cross, and triumphing over death itself was so that we could be *together with Him*. Jesus didn't do these things to lord it over our heads. He did it to bring us closer to Him, which is exactly what Paul tells us a few verses later in the second chapter of Ephesians.

> *"At that time you were without Christ, being aliens from the commonwealth of Israel and strangers from the covenants of promise, having no hope and without God in the world. But now in Christ Jesus you who once were far off have been brought near by the blood of Christ." (Ephesians 2:12-13)*

Again, look at the drastic difference between where we once were and where God has placed us. *When* we were without Christ, we had no hope, no access to the covenants, and no God. *But now.* Now that God has stepped in and saved the day, we have been brought close to Him. We have been given hope. We have been given the covenants. And we have been given God Himself. We are *together* with Him.

Sinner No More

Consider of the implications of what the bible is telling us! We are told that we used to be spiritually dead in our sins, teamed up with the devil and living without God. That would make you a *sinner. But God.* God has made you alive together with Christ. We used to be sinners, but God stepped in and changed us into something new. He lifted us up out of our sinful nature, gave us to a new nature, and sat us next to Jesus Himself. What does that make you? Are you just a sinner, saved by grace?

An emphatic "**NO**"! You are a sinner no longer. I cringe every time a worship song or pastor or Christian book calls me a sinner. Because that is not who I am. Sure, I *was* a sinner. Back in the olden days. But *then* I was saved by grace. And God's grace brought me back to life and made me brand-new. That is the whole point of salvation. To make us new! Not to make the old, broken version of you just good enough to get into heaven, but to make you into someone who rightfully deserves to enter through God's gates.

> *"For if by one man's offense* (Adam) *death reigned through the one, much more those who receive abundance of grace and of the gift of righteousness will reign in life through the One, Jesus Christ. Therefore, as through one man's offense judgment came to all men, resulting in condemnation, even so through one Man's righteous act the free gift came to all men, resulting in justification of life. For as by one man's disobedience many were made sinners, so also by one Man's obedience many will be made righteous."* (Romans 5:17-19)

Did you catch that tidbit about sinners? Adam's transgression brought sin into the world, and infected the human race with a sinful nature, making us by definition *sinners*. But receiving the free gift of grace changes us from *sinful* to *righteous*. That's what the word "justified" means. It means to change from a *sinner* into a *saint*. You once were a sinner who has since been saved by grace, and are therefore now a saint.

This might be a hard concept to grasp. Who knows, maybe you sinned yesterday. Doesn't that make you into a sinner? No, it doesn't, actually. Do you remember what we discussed in the last chapter? Behavior doesn't dictate nature. A dog that walks on its hind legs isn't a human. That works both ways. A golden retriever walking upright isn't a human any more than a human barking is a golden retriever, and a sinner who behaves himself isn't a saint any more than a saint who misbehaves is a sinner.

You may recall the sad state of the church of Corinth. To name just a few problems they were struggling with, they had stopped growing in the things of God and were fighting amongst themselves over petty issues. They were going hog-wild with the gifts of the Spirit, which was freaking out the unsaved population. And worst of all, some guy had entered into a sexual relationship with his step-mom, which the rest of the church thought was adorable. Yet even in this pitiful state, look at how Paul addressed their congregation.

> *"To the church of God which is at Corinth, to those who are sanctified in Christ Jesus, called saints, with all who in every place call on the name of Jesus Christ our Lord, both theirs and ours." (1 Corinthians 1:2)*

Look how he speaks to them. He calls them *saints*. He doesn't say they are sinners. He doesn't say they are pathetic and horrible and hell-bound. He says they are saints. And the criteria he gives for their sainthood is simply that they had "called on the name of Jesus Christ." That's all it takes to be transformed from sinner to saint. Calling on Jesus, thus accepting salvation. Their misbehavior didn't rid them of their sainthood.

Even the guy who is sleeping with his step-mom isn't labeled a sinner.

> *"Therefore purge out the old leaven, that you may be a new lump, since you truly are unleavened..." (1 Corinthians 5:7)*

Don't let the word "leaven" confuse you. It's Paul's metaphorical way of saying "sin." Paul tells them to get rid of the sin in their congregation. Why? Because they aren't really sinful. Their true nature is unleavened, or *non-sinful*. Paul says to them, "Stop acting sinful, because you aren't sinners." And why aren't they sinners?

> *"...For indeed Christ, our Passover, was sacrificed for us." (1 Corinthians 5:7)*

We aren't *saints* because we follow the rules. We are saints because Jesus died to rid us of our sinful nature. It has absolutely nothing to do with our actions. This redemption is entirely a result of Christ's death, resurrection, and ascension. Just as He was crucified, so our sinful nature was put to death. Just as He was resurrected on the third day, so our spirit has been revived by the fresh breath of life. And just as Jesus ascended into the heavens to be seated at the right hand of His Father, so we too sit in the heavenly places with our Dad. We truly are sinners no more.

Free From Sin

This leaves us in a bit of a predicament. You see, it would be very easy to use this knowledge of our righteous nature as an excuse to live in sin. Paul was actually accused of promoting the sinful lifestyle as a viable alternative to righteous living.

> *"What shall we say then? Shall we continue in sin that grace may abound? Certainly not! How shall we who died to sin live any longer in it? ... What then? Shall we sin because we are not under law but under grace? Certainly not!" (Romans 6:1-2, 15)*

Paul spends the entirety of the sixth chapter of Romans disproving this notion. The reason Paul taught that we no longer had a sinful nature wasn't so that we could freely live in sin, but so that we could live a life freed from sin. Remember what Jesus taught in Mark 7. *An evil man brings forth evil things from an evil heart, but a good man brings forth good things from a good heart.* You are good. Your heart is good. Therefore, you are free from a life of sin.

> *"Knowing this, that our old man* (our sin-natured man) *was crucified with Him, that the body of sin* (our sinful nature) *might be done away with, that we should no longer be slaves of sin. For he who has died has been freed from sin." (Romans 6:6-7)*

Righteousness isn't a license to sin. On the contrary, it's the freedom to live a sinless life. The new you, the righteous saint that God transformed you into, is designed to live apart from sin. But since most Christians don't *know* this, we have been stuck in a rut, living a sinful life contrary to our righteous nature. That is why Paul emphasizes that we need to *know* this. You need to know that you are free not just from the consequences of sin, but from sin itself. Your old, sinful nature has passed away; behold, you are new.

This brings us back to that important question that many Christians have wrestled with for years: can you sin and still be righteous? Yes, you can. However, I don't say this with joyful exclamation. We shouldn't *want* to sin. So many Christians accept salvation as a sort of fire insurance, received solely for the purpose of "just in case I'm headed for hell." These Christians will spend their lives trying to see just how much they can live in sin while maintaining their salvation. As I said before, righteousness wasn't designed to give us freedom *to* sin. It was meant to give us freedom *from* sin. We shouldn't just want salvation so that we can escape hell. It should be because we want to be with God. Unfortunately, the church world has spent a great deal of time teaching us of our sin while never teaching us of our freedom, and as a result many Christians have resolved to living their life in bondage to sin.

I had a conversation with an old friend of mine that demonstrates the church's ignorance of righteousness rather well. My friend "Philip" is a successful entrepreneur, and I was in the beginning stages of starting my own business so I called him up to ask for advice. Several minutes into the conversation, we turned to talking about ministry.

"You're still working as a youth pastor, right?" Philip asked me.

"Yes, I am," I replied.

"Great! I have a perfect story for you to share with the kids. It's a great example of how to evangelize."

He had piqued my interest, so I invited him to share his evangelical experience.

"I was talking to a guy at the gym last week. He knows I'm a Christian, and I've tried to talk to him before, but he never really wanted to hear about it. So last week, I just decided to tell him all about Christianity."

I was impressed with his boldness. However, it was Philip's version of the gospel that soon alarmed me.

"I told him, 'Just because I'm a Christian doesn't mean I'm any different than you. I still get drunk from time to time. I still drop the *F-bomb* every now and then. I'm no different than you! I'm just as much of a sinner as you are. The only difference is that I know to say *sorry* when I'm done sinning.'" And that was the conclusion of his evangelistic endeavor.

Quite honestly, I was heartbroken. Philip had learned from his pastor that *bragging* about his sinful lifestyle was the way to win converts. Philip didn't know that his sinful nature had been destroyed. He didn't know that he was righteous. As far as he knew, the only difference between himself and the average sinner was his growing list of apologies. His life looked exactly like the rest of the world.

We are free from the bondage of sin. I've heard that Apple

Computers are immune to viruses. Assuming that's true, consider your spiritual status as that of an Apple Computer. You used to be a PC, and were subject to all sorts of spyware and bugs. But when God got a hold of you, he changed you from a PC to an iMac. You are no longer the victim of spiritual infection. You are impervious to it. Death no longer has a hold on you.

Be Righteous

Fortunately, given that you are reading a Christian book, I'm confident that you don't want to live a life filled with sin. So to close this chapter, I'd like to give you a quick rundown of how to embrace your life of freedom. It all comes down to the new life that Christ has purchased for us.

> *"For the law of the Spirit of life in Christ Jesus has made me free from the law of sin and death." (Romans 8:2)*

Paul teaches extensively that all humans are born with a sinful nature engrafted into our very DNA, which he calls the "law of sin and death." I'd compare this to the legality of slavery in the nineteenth century. In the 1800's, it was completely legal to own slaves. It was incredibly unethical, but slavery was legal nonetheless. However, with the ratification of the Thirteenth Amendment in 1865, slavery became illegal. The legality of slavery was annulled by the Thirteenth Amendment, just as the Spirit of Life nullified the law of sin and death.

Notice that we are "made" free from sin and death. Many times we incorrectly quote Jesus, saying, "Whom the Son *sets* free is free indeed." That's not what Jesus said.

> *"'And you shall know the truth, and the truth shall make you free... therefore if the Son makes you free, you shall be free indeed.'" (John 8:32, 36)*

If a slave were *set* free in the 1800's, he'd still be a slave.

Physically he'd be free, but legally he'd still be in bondage. If an inmate were *set* free from prison, he'd still belong in prison. Being *set* free means that you belong in bondage but have somehow managed to escape, and are now forced to live a life on the run. Jesus didn't *set* anyone free. He *made* you free. If a slave has been *made* free no one has a legal right to enslave him again. His nature has changed. He has been *made* into something new. Jesus *made* you free, meaning that you no longer belong in sin, but instead belong to Him (which is why He placed you in the heavenly places together with Himself).

Know who you are. That is the key to success in your Christian life. Know what God has spoken about you, and you will have an unfair advantage in life. Remember how Jesus overcame His temptation. *"It is written"* (Matthew 4:4, 7, 10). Jesus knew what God had spoken, and armed with that knowledge He spoke those truths in the face of the devil himself, and came out victorious every time. You too will need to arm yourself with the truth of God's word. Here's some more ammo to keep in your arsenal of righteous truth.

> *"'Therefore, O king, let my advice be acceptable to you; break off your sins by being righteous...'"* (Daniel 4:27)

The Babylonian king's sins had caught up with him, and he was at risk of receiving the results of a life of sin. That was when he turned to Daniel for help. And Daniel's advice? "Be righteous." Even under the old covenant, the path to overcoming sin wasn't to relying on your own strength. It was to embrace God's free gift of righteousness. Only when you have been made righteous can you ever hope to live apart from sin.

Finally, Jesus' interaction with the adulterous woman has taught me much about living a holy life. We all know the story. A woman has been caught committing adultery, "in the very act." The Pharisees bring her to Jesus, hoping to force him into condemning this young woman. He slyly rebukes them, asking who among them is qualified to pass judgment on her, which scatters the accusatory crowds. After the masses have fled, Jesus and the woman are left alone. Jesus turns to her and says,

> *"Neither do I condemn you; go and try really hard not to sin."*

No, that's not quite right.

> *"Neither do I condemn you; go and read the popular Christian book,* 12 Steps on How Not to Sin.*"*

That's not what He said, either.

> *"Neither do I condemn you; go and sin no more."* (John 8:11)

Hear the words that came forth from Jesus' mouth. "Go and *sin no more.*" He tells this Jewish woman that she has the ability to live the rest of her days without committing a single sin. So often, Christians make seemingly humble statements like, "I sin thousands of times every day" and, "It's impossible not to sin." Jesus thought differently. Jesus seemed to think that we could live a life free from sin. And He'd know; after all, He did it. He lived His entire life without committing a single sin. Then He invited us to live in the same exact way, complete with a new nature, together with Him.

I don't care what popular Christian music says. I don't care what famous pastors say. I care solely about what God says. And God said you are new. He said that all of the old garbage that used to define your life has been dealt with, once and for all. He said you are alive, that you are good, that you are righteous, and that you never have to sin again.

Without a shadow of a doubt, you are no longer a sinner.

You are a saint.

Final Thoughts

Before moving on to the next chapter, pray this prayer out loud right now.

Dad, I know that I used to be a sinner. I used to be spiritually dead, without hope and without You. But that is not who I am any longer. Thank You Jesus that I have been made alive together with You. Thank You that I have been made free from the sinful nature, and that I never have to sin again. I declare before heaven and earth that I am a righteous child of God. Sin has no power over me! I am a new creation, made in the perfect image of God.

Amen.

Small Group Questions

1. How does this chapter relate to what you're currently reading in the bible?

2. What did Peter have in Acts 3? Do you have it too?

3. In what three ways are we "together" with Christ?

4. Are you a sinner or a saint? Why?

5. Should Christians live in sin?

6. Do you have the power to overcome sin in your life?

7. Read Ephesians 2:4-6. What is one notable thing about this verse?

8. What was the main point of this chapter?

5
Like God

"'Blessed are the poor in spirit, for theirs is the kingdom of heaven.'" (Matthew 5:3)

I'm sure most of us are familiar with this passage. It adorns Christian T-shirts, youth group walls, throw pillows that your grandma knit herself. These are the world-renowned beatitudes, the introduction to Jesus' first recorded and most famous teaching, the Sermon on the Mount.

And this is how we typically read the beatitudes.

"The poor in spirit receive the kingdom of heaven, those who mourn are comforted, the meek inherit the earth, the hungry are filled," and so on and so forth. It makes for a great list of conditional statements, which is exactly how Wikipedia (the ultimate source of knowledge) describes them.

The poor in spirit: *theirs is the kingdom*
Those who mourn: *they shall be comforted*
The meek: *they shall inherit the earth*
Those who hunger and thirst for righteousness: *they shall be filled*
The merciful: *they shall obtain mercy*
The pure in heart: *they shall see God*
The peacemakers: *they shall be called sons of God*
Those persecuted for righteousness' sake: *theirs is the kingdom*

In our attempt to be efficient and standardize the teachings of Christ, we have converted this messy, jumbled paragraph into a simple, concise list. And now we have our cookie cutter bible study, our kids' ministry poster, our thirty second YouTube video, which has effectively been robbed of all power and meaning.

You see, what we have done here is what we so often do. We perform a sleight of hand magic trick, seeing only what we want to see and leaving out the rest. The church has done this for centuries. Unfortunately, what we have left out is the most important part. It's the basis for every sermon Jesus subsequently taught and without it, the church will be cut off at the knees. Correction: the church *has* been cut off at the knees. We've crippled ourselves by ignoring what was right in front of our eyes.

I assume that now you're pulling a "Where's Waldo?" flipping through your reference bible to see what exactly we've left out. Rather than keep you waiting in the excruciating uncertainty that is now consuming your mind, I'll show you exactly what I'm talking about.

> *"And seeing the multitudes, He went up on a mountain, and when He was seated His disciples came to Him. Then He opened His mouth and taught them, saying: 'Blessed...'"* (Matthew 5:1-3)

I love the suspense that Matthew builds here in anticipation of Jesus' sermon. The masses approach. Jesus leads them. Then He sits down. The disciples huddle in close. He opens His mouth. And a wellspring of life gushes forth from His lips.

"Blessed."

This is the word that begins His most famous sermon. Of all the things He could've said, "love," "life," "God," or "tithe," He chose to call us "blessed." This is what we've been missing for centuries. This is what has been left out of our doctrinal lists and exegesis. This is what we've overlooked, again and again and again.

Where's Waldo? He's blessed.

The Blessing of the Lord

The reason this word is so easy to ignore is because it doesn't really *mean* anything to us. Consider it officially added to the Christianese Dictionary. We just don't care about blessings in our culture. This word doesn't mean anything to us. It's just something we say when someone sneezes within fifteen feet of us, or what we say to a fellow church-goer we've had enough of.

"Well, I've got to go. The wife is waiting. Bless you, brother." Then we book it to the door before the meaningless blessing can be returned. Blessings simply don't matter to us.

When I first met Cheyne's father, he was hesitant to welcome what he accurately characterized as "the hairy man" into his family. But Cheyne persisted, so he invited me along to attend an office party with him one Saturday afternoon. At the time, he was working for a well-known pastor, so once we arrived, we headed straight for the famous clergyman.

"Pastor," my soon-to-be father-in-law said, "this is Garrett, my daughter's... friend."

The pastor's eyes locked in with mine, and as we shook hands he reached up and patted me on the shoulder. "Bless you, child," he said to me.

I had no idea how to respond. Bless you? What did that even mean? I hadn't sneezed. At least I didn't think I had. What was I supposed to do? How was I supposed to respond?

Without thinking, I reached out my left hand and patted him on his shoulder in return. "No no no, bless *you*," I responded. I thought it was pretty witty. Cheyne giggled; her dad shook his head in embarrassment; the pastor stared awkwardly at me, as if he had never received a "blessing" from a complete stranger before. That made two of us.

In western culture, we just don't appreciate what a blessing means. But consider this. The highlight of the book of Genesis was the declaration of blessings. Jacob and Esau went head-to-head over Isaac's blessing. Jacob went as far as to betray his brother, deceive his father, then retreat to a life as a renegade outlaw in the hope of receiving his father's blessing. Esau, much like us, didn't seem to mind and let it slip away. But in Jesus' world these so-called blessings were somewhat of a big deal, which would explain why God directed Jesus to begin His most important teaching with that simple word: *blessed*.

I believe it's of the utmost importance to note that the scripture doesn't say, "God *blesses* the poor in spirit, for theirs is the kingdom." This isn't a verb. It's not something that God is performing for you. It's a declaration of *who you are*. "Blessed *are* the poor in spirit."

You, my friend, are blessed. Quite blessed, actually.

But what does that word even mean? Yes, maybe you can admit that you are a blessed individual. But this is just some esoteric word that lacks any real meaning to us. Scramble your brain, and the best definition you can probably come up with is "lucky," maybe "fortunate." That hardly scratches the surface.

The word translated "blessed" comes from the Greek word *makarios*, which literally means "dead." I find this particularly humorous, seeing how I just spent the last two chapters convincing you that you were, in fact, alive. Here I am, writing a book about how you have been brought back to life when the Son of God shows up and discredits me with a single word.

Not exactly.

You see, although this word literally means "dead," it doesn't actually *mean* "dead." What it means is "beyond the cares of this life." The Greeks used this word to describe those that had died and had traveled to the world of their gods. As they were dead, the petty things of this world, like money, clothes, food, and weather, simply weren't an issue anymore. They were free from the limits of this human life and were on their way to paradise (or so they thought).

The Greeks also used this word *makarios* to describe the highest echelon of society. Just as the dead were beyond the cares of this life, so were the rich and fabulous. They had all of their needs met, they had access to everything they could ever want, and they basically lived as gods among men, not needing to fret over the small stuff.

Of course, the most common usage of this word *makarios* was in reference to the Greek gods themselves. As deities, they had absolutely no fear of death. They would never experience any consequences of death, be it physical, mental, or spiritual. All in all, they were completely free from the pangs of death.

Thus the word *makarios* was most often used to describe the gods. In fact, it was actually used to distinguish the gods from men.

> *"However, let these two themselves be witnesses before the **blessed** gods and mortal men..." (The Iliad, Book I)*

In this ancient Greek classic, the blind poet Homer invokes the word *blessed* to describe just how different the gods were from mere men. The gods had absolutely everything they could ever need or desire. The world was at their fingertips, and death itself had no power over them.

And this word, jam-packed with all of this tremendous meaning and history and mythos, is the word Jesus chose to describe you. Of all the words in Christ's infinite vocabulary, He picked this one. You still may not see it, but the people Jesus spoke to certainly did. It's quite evident by the way they lived their lives. No wonder they forsook all to follow Him! They forfeited all of their material possessions, and yet God always provided an abundant supply. They surrendered their bodies to be beaten and persecuted, trusting God would restore them to perfect health. And just as Jesus had instructed, they gave up their own lives, essentially "dying" to self, that they would experience true life here on earth. They weren't just lucky or fortunate. No, it was much more than that. They lived the blessed life of God Himself.

Poor in Spirit

We're making fantastic progress. We're halfway through the chapter, and we've covered *one* word. What a blessing. Let's read further into the chapter.

> *"'Blessed are the poor in spirit, for theirs is the kingdom of heaven.'" (Matthew 5:3)*

The point is clear: if you want access to God's kingdom, you must be poor in spirit. And probably all around poverty-stricken. Just be deprived in every area of life. Then you can rest assured that God will be with you. Empty yourself, have absolutely nothing worth anything, and life will be grand.

At least that's what we've been taught for years. But I have some shocking news for you. You're not supposed to be poor in spirit. Not anymore, anyway.

For the sake of clarity, I'm going to suggest that we word "poor in spirit" a little differently. We are going to define it as *spiritually lacking*. "Blessed are those who are spiritually lacking, for theirs is the kingdom." Two thousand years ago when Jesus preached this, who were the poor in spirit? Who was spiritually lacking?

The multitudes that flocked to him certainly were. Whatever their financial situation or social standing, they were spiritually dead. I feel it is safe to call that a spiritual deficiency. But what about the religious elite, those Pharisees and Sadducees and scribes who spent years trying to sabotage Jesus in vain? Were they spiritually lacking, or were they prospering in the things of God?

Obviously, they were spiritually poor as well. In fact, *everybody* on planet earth was spiritually poor. As we discussed extensively in the previous chapters, all were infected with Adam's sinful nature. All were spiritually dead. All were separated from God and thus were without hope in this world. Every single one of them was poor in spirit.

> *"Blessed are everyone, for theirs is the kingdom of heaven."*

That couldn't possibly be what Jesus meant. After all, if that were the case He could have made life easy for all of us and said, "You're all blessed! Congrats!" So what does it mean to be poor in spirit? Turning to the gospels will provide some insight.

> *"And when the scribes and Pharisees saw Him eating with the tax collectors and sinners, they said to His disciples, 'How is it that He eats and drinks with tax collectors and sinners?' When Jesus heard it, He said to them, 'Those who are well have no need of a physician, but those who are sick. I did not come to call the righteous, but sinners, to repentance.'" (Mark 2:16-17)*

Jesus makes two crazy characterizations here. He implies that the Pharisees, those who would spend decades persecuting Him and His church, were already "well" and "righteous." Jesus claims that He was there only for the sick and sin-filled, not the well and righteous. Why would Jesus call the Pharisees righteous, when that positively could not have been the truth?

Simple. They weren't really righteous. They were *self*-righteous. They considered themselves the cream of the crop, the head honchos, the religiously satisfied that had no need for any help or intervention whatsoever. And Jesus makes it a point to explain that until one *acknowledges* their own spiritual poverty they cannot receive His blessing. The Pharisees definitely were not *well*, but they were too proud and dumb to go to the Doctor for healing.

> *"Blessed are those who acknowledge their spiritual poverty, for theirs is the kingdom."*

In this passage, Jesus isn't describing the condition of a saved individual. He's giving instructions on how to access God's Kingdom. You need to be poor in spirit to *get in*. But once you're in, you are poor no more.

I can prove this.

> *"For thus says the High and Lofty One Who inhabits eternity, whose name is Holy: 'I dwell in the high and holy place, with him who has a contrite and humble spirit, to revive the spirit*

of the humble, and to revive the heart of the contrite ones.'"
(Isaiah 57:15)

This passage is a popular cross-reference for those who insist that we remain spiritually poor for all eternity. "See," they say, "we must be contrite in spirit to be with God. We must be spiritually poor."

But I want you to notice the condition of a contrite spirit. They are in need of reviving. That means they are dead. Just as Jesus said hundreds of years after Isaiah penned this manuscript, God can only revive those who admit their poor condition and come to Him for help. When a contrite and humble spirit approaches God, He revives them. He gives them new life. And they are dead no longer.

When you think it through, being poor in spirit is absolutely incompatible with blessedness. To be blessed is to be rich, carefree, godlike. Can you truly be blessed if you're constantly lacking? And even if that were so, the result of your spiritual poverty is that God *gives you the kingdom*. I haven't been given an earthly kingdom yet, but I'd imagine that if any kingdom were handed over to me, I'd be pretty well off. Let's not attempt to live this life as a spiritually poor individual. Instead, let us thrive in the blessings of blessedness that God has blessed us with. You are blessed. Your spiritual poverty has been removed, tossed into the abyss along with spiritual death and sin.

Like Father, Like Son

I feel it necessary to clarify something right now. Just because you aren't spiritually poor doesn't mean that you're hot stuff all on your own. Fall into that trap and you'll be resting in the company of the Pharisees and Sadducees. Sure, you may be spiritually rich, but you didn't fill that bank account on your own. You just have Daddy's credit card.

"And my God shall supply all your need according to His

Like God

riches in glory by Christ Jesus." (Philippians 4:19)

Think of Bruce Wayne. The man is *loaded*. The so-called "Prince of Gotham," the world is his oyster. He lives in the biggest mansion this side of Metropolis, drives the fanciest cars, does and buys whatever he wants. Heck, in *Batman Begins*, he bought a hotel on a whim just so he could swim in the fountain. He gets whatever he wants.

Who pays for all of these extravagant (and incredibly irresponsible) purchases? He does. But with whose money? His dad's. You see, although he has a VISA strapped to that utility belt that will never run dry, he'd have absolutely *nothing* if it weren't for his father. In fact, without his father's money, not only would he be unable to live as Bruce Wayne, he'd be unable to moonlight as Batman. It's all contingent on his inheritance from Dr. Thomas Wayne, MD.

In the same way, you have *nothing* without God. But luckily, you're not without God. Therefore, you have uninhibited access to all of God's riches. Though you're one hundred percent dependent on God, you are an heir of His Kingdom. Just like those fortunate enough to have borne the title of *makarios* before you, you have everything you could ever want or need. That is the unfair advantage I've been talking about.

I hope the point is becoming clear. With every brick I lay in this book, I'm building in you a confidence in your heavenly Dad. I'm not making this stuff up. This is what God has said about you. You are alive. You are good. You are righteous. You are *blessed*. That means you get to live *like God*.

Now, I've alluded to this several times, but in case you missed it, I'll say it loud and clear. **You are like God.** Okay, slow down. Before you take up rocks to stone me, allow me to demonstrate.

> *"Therefore the Jews sought all the more to kill Him, because He not only broke the Sabbath, but also said that God was His Father, making Himself equal with God." (John 5:18)*

According to Jewish culture, father and son were considered to be on the same level. The Jews were offended by Jesus not because of His blatant disregard for their traditions, but because He claimed to be God's Son. And in their understanding, being a son of God meant you were just like God.

Surely the Jews were mistaken. How did Jesus weigh in on the issue?

> *"[Jesus said], 'I and My Father are one.' Then the Jews took up stones again to stone Him... Jesus answered them, 'Is it not written in your law, "I said, 'You are gods'"? If He called them gods, to whom the word of God came (and the Scripture cannot be broken), do you say of Him whom the Father sanctified and sent into the world, "You are blaspheming," because I said, "I am the Son of God"?'" (John 10:30-31, 34-36)*

Jesus uses the phrases "I am the Son of God" and "I and My Father are one" interchangeably. This idea that being related to God makes you just like Him isn't a cultural thing; it's a truth thing. And it makes a ton of sense when you think about it. The Genesis account of creation repeatedly claims that every living thing brings forth after its own kind. Birds make birds, cows make cows, trees make trees. So what does God make?

Again, put down the stones. I am certainly not claiming that I am God. That'd be an incredibly silly thing to say. All I am saying is that I'm *like* God. All the way back in the garden, God declared that He wanted His kids to be "in His likeness and in His image." From the very beginning we were intended to be just like Him. But then mankind fell, and we took on the likeness and image of sin. But when you finally get over your pride and admit that you are spiritually poor and that you can't do life on your own, God sweeps in and adopts you into His family. No longer spiritually poor, no longer spiritually dead, you are finally *like Him*, just as He planned from the beginning.

In fact, Jesus goes as far as to say that *you are gods* (little "g" gods). This is a direct quote from the 82nd Psalm. Go back and read that psalm. God is speaking to His people, whom He declares "are gods" (literally meaning *gods, divine ones, godlike ones*), simply because they "are children of the Most High." However, they don't seem to understand this concept, and as a result they refuse to act like it. Instead of behaving like God as they were called to do, in their ignorance they choose to live like men, and ultimately "die like men." It's a sad tale. They were called to be like God but refused to accept it, and ultimately never lived up to their potential, their calling, their destiny.

This leaves us with a choice to make. We can accept God at His Word, or we can reject it. Abraham, Peter, David, and Paul all chose to accept this divine calling; Koran, Sapphira, Ahab, and the Pharisees rejected it.

This brings to mind a quote from the movie *Kill Bill: Volume 2*, which is packed with Quentin Tarrantino-esque violence and Quentin Tarrantino-esque language.

> *"Now, a staple of the superhero mythology is, there's the superhero and there's the alter ego. Batman is actually Bruce Wayne, Spider-Man is actually Peter Parker. When that character wakes up in the morning, he's Peter Parker. He has to put on a costume to become Spider-Man. And it is in that characteristic Superman stands alone. Superman didn't become Superman. Superman was born Superman. When Superman wakes up in the morning, he's Superman. His alter ego is Clark Kent. His outfit with the big red "S," that's the blanket he was wrapped in as a baby when the Kents found him. Those are his clothes. What Kent wears – the glasses, the business suit – that's his costume. That's the costume Superman wears to blend in with us. Clark Kent is how Superman views us. And what are the characteristics of Clark Kent? He's weak... he's unsure of himself... he's a coward. Clark Kent is Superman's critique on the whole human race."*
> (Kill Bill: Volume 2)

Ah, so, the point emerges. Who are you going to be? The choice is yours. You can embrace your divine nature and live the life God has called you to live, or you can surrender to a menial life of bleak humanness. That is what the Corinthians had done.

> *"For you are still carnal. For where there are envy, strife, and divisions among you, are you not carnal and behaving like mere men?" (1 Corinthians 3:3)*

The word "carnal" means *human*. Paul is rebuking them for acting human. Why? Because they aren't human. Not anymore, anyway. They are *divine*. They are *godlike*. They are children of the Most High. Mere human living isn't fitting for a child of God. You are called to enormous things. You are mighty. You are tremendous. You are greater than you realize.

So what's it going to be?

> *"I call heaven and earth as witnesses today against you, that I have set before you life and death, blessing and cursing; therefore choose life, that both you and your descendents may live." (Deuteronomy 30:19)*

Final Thoughts

Wow. I find the things we've discussed in this chapter incredibly exciting! Before moving on to the next chapter, let's talk to our Dad about what we've learned, and ask Him to continually reveal these truths to us through His Word.

Dad, what an exhilarating thing to recognize that I truly have been made in Your divine image. What a privilege to know You, to talk with You, to be like You. I thank You that every single day, I am more and more like You. Today, I give you permission to invade every part of my life, and to teach me how to live like You. I will think Your thoughts. I will speak Your words. I will live like You live. Thank You that when people see me, they see You living in me. Thank You that I am a blessed child of the Most High God. I love You, Dad!

Amen!

Small Group Questions

1. How does this chapter relate to what you're currently reading in the bible?

2. Why do you think blessings were so important to the Jewish people?

3. In what ways does the word "blessed" describe you?

4. Does being the heir to a rich parent make you rich or poor? Why?

5. Does being a child of God make you like God? In what ways?

6. How should Christians look to the unsaved?

7. Read John 10:34-36. What is one notable thing about this verse?

8. What was the main point of this chapter?

6

The Dream House

The master bathroom had two doors. That's the reason we didn't buy that house.

Okay, maybe that wasn't the *only* reason. But it was definitely a big reason.

After almost five years of marriage, Cheyne and I are finally ready to purchase our first home. That's kind of a big deal. I mean, how many half-million dollar purchases does the average family make in their life? I don't intend on buying a yacht any time soon, so a house will most likely be the most expensive thing I ever buy. We've been searching for a couple of months now, and let me tell you, you never really know what things are important to you until someone asks you how many *hundreds of thousands* of dollars you are willing to pay for them.

There was one house that seemed pretty good. Sure, it was a tad bit too far from our church, and yes, the neighborhood didn't have paved roads, and yeah, our neighbor had a tireless pickup truck resting – rusting – on his front lawn... okay, okay, the house wasn't the obvious pick of the litter. But the straw that broke the camel's back was the upstairs bathroom. It had two doors: one adjoined to the master bedroom, and the other to what would potentially be our daughter's bedroom.

That was just too much for me. After all, a man's bathroom is his sanctuary. It's where I get most of my reading done. It's where I became proficient in Angry Birds, and a plethora of other mobile games. It's my man-cave. A man needs to feel at home in his bathroom, and I just wasn't willing to compromise on that. A longer commute was one thing. Tacky neighbors and dirt roads and living out in no-man's-land were all tolerable. But I wasn't willing to share my bathroom with a teenage girl. All her stuff would be lying around. Make-up paraphernalia, hair-straighteners, hair-curlers, *other things…*

Maybe I was being slightly fickle and a little overdramatic, but this is my future house we're talking about. I might have to live there for the next eighty years of my life. And if I'm going to make the largest investment of my life, I think it's fair to be a little picky about it. And I intend to be just as picky as I can get away with.

However, I don't actually intend to live in my first house for eighty years. Someday, I hope to design and build a dream house for my family. There will be many details and intricacies that cater to our every whim, but there is one such feature that I am particularly proud of, and excited to bring to fruition. Brace yourself for this. Awesomeness is about to assault your mind.

Somewhere deep within the bowels of our future home, behind a bookshelf or piano or flat-screen television, there will be a secret room. Growing up, our kids will be entirely unaware of its existence. Within this room, we will hang framed newspaper articles. *Fake* newspaper articles. *Heavily photo-shopped* fake newspaper articles. These articles will feature my wife and me donning superhero outfits. Bold letters will headline these articles, with such epic statements as "*G-Man* and his beautiful sidekick, *The Scarlet Thunder*, Save Citizens Yet Again!" and "Super Team Arrives Just in Nick of Time!" (I'm aware that I need to come up with better names.)

There will also be costumes hand-stitched by Cheyne and me, displayed in giant glass cases. Maybe some futuristic weapons lining the walls, mementos from our faux past. Heirlooms of a time that had never been. Hopefully a classic car as well, complete with a custom paint job, rocket boosters, and my hero insignia.

My young children will grow up oblivious to our fictional back-story. But one fateful day when my kids approach roughly ten years of age, they will notice a beam of light protruding from underneath the bookshelf, accidentally left on. They will grow suspicious, they might even inquire, and eventually, they will find their way into our fortress of solitude. There they will stumble upon our alter-egos. They will think that we used to be superheroes.

And what a great day that will be.

That is the tale of my future dream house. And it is in that house that I intend to dwell all the rest of my days.

Temples

The Apostle Paul asked the church of Corinth a very interesting question.

> *"Do you not know that your body is the temple of the Holy Spirit who is in you?" (1 Corinthians 6:19)*

How do you think the Corinthians would answer that question? For that matter, how do you think *any* Christian would answer that question?

"Yes! No duh, I know that. Obviously, the Holy Spirit is in me. Who doesn't know that?"

I think you'd be hard-pressed to find a Christian who wasn't aware of this fact. The Corinthians certainly were. Read through Paul's first letter to the church at Corinth and you will discover that spiritual gifts were rampant in that city. This was a church well acquainted with the Holy Spirit. An emphatic "Yes!" would have issued forth from their lips in response to Paul's question.

What exactly was Paul getting at? Paul was a smart enough guy to know not to waste our time with trivial questions. What point was Paul trying to get across?

Exactly what he said. *"Do you not know that the Holy Spirit dwells within you?"* You see, the church at Corinth was filled with parishioners who knew that God dwelt in their mortal bodies, but they didn't actually *know* it. It was painfully obvious by the way they lived. Sure, they openly acknowledged that they had been informed of this biblical truth, but it had never progressed beyond head knowledge.

When I was nine, I walked over to Nick's house, my friend who was fifteen at the time. I knocked on the door, and when he answered I asked if he could play. Probably wanting to let down the little kid easily, he told me he was working on his math homework, and unless I knew the square root of 81, I couldn't come in. He closed the door, and I walked home.

Five minutes later there was a knock at his door, and when he opened it I was waiting for him.

"Nine!" I proudly exclaimed, and walked right into his house in triumphant victory. During that five minute interval, I had gone home and asked my mother the answer to his impossible problem. Now, I knew that the square root of 81 was 9, but I didn't really *know* it. It was just a fact that I had overheard and repeated, but it wasn't a reality to me.

That was as far as the Corinthians' knowledge extended. They could parrot this fact, this concept, of the Holy Spirit living inside of them, but they didn't really believe it. It wasn't a reality to them. If it were, they would have talked differently. They would have acted differently. They would have *lived* differently.

And sadly, many Christians fall into this same category. Ask them if they are temples of the Holy Spirit and they can answer correctly. But honestly, do they really believe that? Are you consciously aware that God Himself, in all of His magnificence and glory and power, is inside of you *right now*?

Greater Than John

This neglect of the Holy Spirit's current residence becomes clearer when you hear how people talk about the Old Testament saints.

"Man, Moses *talked with God*. When I get to heaven, I'm going to have to ask him what that was like."

"David was crazy legit! I can't wait to ask him what it was like to dwell *with God*!"

Listen. Those saints of old, while epic and amazing and incredibly awesome, are going to be lining up around the block to talk to *you* when you enter through those pearly gates!

"Wait, you mean that God actually *lived* inside of you?"

"Hold the phone! *You* were the temple of God? What was that like, to have God *inside* of you?"

Read through the Bible, and you will see that those who lived under the Old Covenant had *nothing* like what we have. It's easy to read those stories without realizing exactly what was taking place. For instance, after God appeared to Cain, more than *five hundred years* passed before God showed up again. God just wasn't as readily available in those days. Almost a millennium passed between Enoch and Noah. God's interactions with mankind in those dark days were far and in between.

Even the relationship between God and Abraham was sporadic. We read the story of Abraham and think this all took place in a highly relational week of time. But those few interactions recorded in Genesis happened over the course of several decades. God showed up and revealed Himself to Abraham. Then several years went by before God showed up again.

And the thing I find absolutely crazy about this is that those very few and very distant conversations between God and Abraham were enough to keep Abraham going. A word from God once every decade was enough to keep Abraham faithful. And yet we have unfettered access to our Dad, and He still has to work overtime to keep us in line.

From the time of man's fall until the time of Moses, God did not dwell *in* man. He also didn't dwell *with* man. He had simply revealed Himself *to* man.

Then came Moses, the law, and the liberated nation of Israel. God instructed Moses to build Him a tabernacle so He could dwell *with* men. During those times, wandering through the wilderness and eventually into the Promised Land, God was in their midst, among His people. His people had access to Him, albeit through the ordained priestly order. During the days of the Judges, God was *with* His people. Throughout David's tenure as king, God was *with* His people. For the rest of the Old Testament, God was *with* His people. But He was never *in* His people.

But all of that changed when the veil was torn.

Do you understand what this means? It means that you have it better than Abraham had it. You have it better than Moses and David and Elijah. Heck, you have it better than John the Baptist. Jesus Himself said that "the least in the Kingdom of Heaven is greater than John" (Matthew 11:11). Now John was the greatest of the Old Covenant prophets. By Jesus' own account, John exceeded all of the patriarchs and judges and kings and priests. And yet, for some inexplicable reason, Jesus seemed to think that *you* were greater than John. What on earth could possibly make you, little old you, greater than John?

> "He who is <u>in you</u> is greater than he who is in the world." (1 John 4:4)

Not only do you have God revealed to you as Enoch and Abraham, not only do you have God with you as Elisha and Gideon, you have God dwelling within you. I don't know if you own dancing shoes, but I suggest you throw on a pair right about now.

Paul felt compelled to question the Corinthians about this. *Do you really know?* God. Actual God. You know, that Guy who made *everything in the universe.* He lives inside of you. For thousands of years that was His endgame. When He appeared to Abraham those few times He was picturing the day when He could live inside of you. When He took up camp with the wandering Israelites in the desert He had you in mind. When He moved into the Holy of Holies He knew it was only going to be a temporary stay. You were His final destination. You were His dream home.

Sometimes I'll just sit and stare at my hands, and say to myself, "The Holy Spirit flows through my veins." I find it exhilarating to meditate upon this reality, that God Himself lives within me. And to think, that was His plan all along.

> "To [the saints] God willed to make known what are the riches of the glory of this mystery among the Gentiles: which is Christ in you, the hope of glory." (Colossians 1:27)

That "mystery of life" that so much of the world is worrying about? That evasive metaphysical construct that philosophers and poets and dreamers and scientists have been trying to solve for ages? Here it is. Drum roll, please.

> *"Christ in you, the hope of glory."*

God making his home within man. There it is.

Far Above

How would your life be different if you could come to terms with the fact that God is within you? This isn't the pantheistic theology of the hippies. God isn't in everyone, but He is in you. Would your life look different if you truly believed that *The God*, the Alpha and the Omega, Yahweh Himself, was contained underneath your skin? What things would you do if this was true? My goodness, what things *wouldn't* you do if this were true?

You may not realize it, but this is the gospel. *God is in you.* Everything God did since the creation was for this purpose. The reason Jesus came to earth and died for your sins was so God could make His abode in you. Remember the parable Jesus told concerning the wineskins.

> *"'And no one puts new wine into old wineskins; or else the new wine bursts the wineskins, the wine is spilled, and the wineskins are ruined. But new wine must be put into new wineskins.'"* (Mark 2:22)

The reason God made you into a new creation was so you would be a worthy vessel for Him to live within. Look back at the detailed description of salvation in Ezekiel.

> *"'I will give you a new heart and put a new spirit within you; I will take the heart of stone out of your flesh and give you a*

heart of flesh. I will put My Spirit within you and cause you to walk in My statutes, and you will keep My judgments and do them.'" (Ezekiel 36:26-27)

The reason God put a new heart and a new spirit within you was so He could then come take up residence in that body of yours. I sure hope this is becoming clear. *God really does live inside of you.* Right now as you are reading this book, God is dwelling within you. When you're in line at the grocery store, God is there, with you and in you. When you're stuck in traffic, God is stuck in you.

Consider the implications of this magnificent reality. *God is in you.* I realize that I've already said that, but it bears repeating. *God is in you. God is in you. God is in you.* Let that sink in. Chew on it over and over again. Allow yourself to become saturated with this truth. *God is in you.* This isn't something to take lightly. It's not just a sentence on a page of a book. Don't read it, think it cool, and then move on. Dwell on it. Become well acquainted with this absolute fact. Believe it. *God is in you.*

Just imagine what this could mean for you. If you were stranded on an island without a pastor, bible, or internet connection, and only knew of one single truth, that God actually did dwell within you, what conclusions would you jump to? If you knew nothing except that the God who invented bananas and waterfalls and bumble bees and the Milky Way Galaxy lived inside of you, what would you assume about your life? If you had never heard a so-called biblical scholar explain why God isn't as grand and powerful and awesome as you had hoped, how would you interpret this profound information regarding God's home address? Would you shrink away from the pressures of this world? Would you settle for less than you hoped you could have? Would you retreat into a menial existence of helplessness and defeat?

Paul saw how imperative it was to remind the church of this truth. He asked the Corinthian church repeatedly, *"Don't you know that you are God's temple? Do you not understand that the Holy Spirit is in you?"* In his letter to the Ephesians, he prayed over and over again that this reality would sink in.

> *"I do not cease to give thanks for you, making mention of you in my prayers… that you may know… what is the exceeding greatness of His power toward us who believe." (Ephesians 1:16, 18-19)*

The word "toward" is the Greek word *eis*, which is overwhelmingly translated as "in" throughout the New Testament. *God's power is in you.* Now, many Christians might surrender to this truth, but they'll dilute it with excuses and self-degradation until it means practically nothing. *Sure, God is in us, but only to help me cope with the troubles of this world. I mean, who am I?* Do not believe this lie! Read the words that Paul wrote to describe God's power within you. He didn't just say, "Yes, God's power is in you." He called it *exceedingly great*. I dare you to look those two words up in a concordance, just to get a grasp on how big God's power within you really is. God put His Holy Spirit inside of you, and with it, His exceedingly great power.

Paul then spends the next four verses describing how grandiose this power really is, as if in anticipation of scholarly and secular explanations to the contrary.

> *"…the exceeding greatness of His power in us who believe, according to the working of His mighty power which He worked in Christ when He raised Him from the dead and seated Him at His right hand in the heavenly places, far above all principality and power and might and dominion, and every name that is named, not only in this age but also in that which is to come. And He put all things under His feet, and gave Him to be head over all things to the church." (Ephesians 1:19-22)*

Read that again. No really, I insist.

Forgive Paul of his grammatically-infuriating run-on sentences, and soak up this powerful description of God within you. The same power that brought Jesus from death to life and ascended Him to the right hand of His Father dwells within your arms and legs. This unfathomable power which flows directly from God into you is not just *above* all the powers that exist in this world, but *far above* it. And look at what this power is above. Everything. Absolutely everything. And not only everything that currently exists, but everything that will *ever* exist. Just as every current disease, economic recession, homework assignment, and renegade army is beneath this God who dwells within you, so every *future* disease, recession, assignment, and army will be forced to bow its knee and submit to this God of ours. And you, my friend, are where He lives.

But Paul still didn't stop at that. That's what I love about reading Paul's letters. Once he started talking about how great and wonderful and splendid and infinite his God was, you just couldn't shut him up. So he continued, explaining that this power (of which you are completely saturated with) put *all things* under the feet of Jesus. How many things? All of 'em. Every single thing must yield to this power.

And not just every *thing*. You see, when Paul originally wrote this letter, he didn't put the word "thing" there. It was added into the text when the Greek epistle was translated into the English language for the sake of clarity. This means that not only is this God-power within you far above any *thing* you might come across, but it's far above things that aren't even things.

Doc Brown's flux capacitor, for instance. That's not even a thing. You still have power over it. Kryptonite. That's not a thing either. You're still above it. Anything and everything that is or is not really even a thing, things that may or may not exist in the future, every person, place and thing, every verb and adjective and preposition, every theory and philosophy and abstract idea that anyone has ever thought about, doodled, or dreamed up, *all*... the power of God is far above it. And that God, El Shaddai, the God-Who-Is-More-Than-Enough, is in you at this precise moment.

And then God gave that power, that authority, that life, over to His church. The church. You and me and that goofy youth pastor with the silly hat. Us saints. That's where God hid that treasure. In us Christians, who bicker and complain about the economy and argue about exactly how we are supposed to baptize converts. This is exactly why Paul told the church to stop acting like mere men. We are too important to be stopped by a democrat or republican president. You are God's temple, after all. God lives inside of you. *God is in you right now.*

It makes perfect sense when you think it through. Imagine Bill Gates purchased a home in your town. At first, the house was old and dilapidated and all around *terrible*. But Bill put most of his money into it. It was a very costly venture, but sure enough, he turned that old shack around. He added a ton of square-footage, a dozen walk-in closets, pools and jacuzzis and tennis courts. The property was large and well-designed and quite impressive. It'd have to be. After all, it belongs to Bill Gates. This new mansion passed all of its inspections and surpassed all the building standards required by law. Finally, his dream house was complete.

Would Bill move in, or would he move on? This mansion is his pride and joy, after all. He put a lot of blood, sweat, and tears into the thing. You better believe he's gonna move in! And he probably wouldn't be satisfied with an empty house. He would most likely furnish the place with all of the newest high-end gear. Ceiling speakers, security systems, thousand-inch flat screens, Lamborghinis and Maseratis and Aston Martins, pool tables, maybe even the original Iron Man suit. He would deck the place out. He'd make that place heaven on earth.

Do you see where this is going?

Let's not be a people that denies these truths any longer. Let's stop making excuses and theological theories about why what God said isn't really true. Instead, let's embrace this God, this holy Sojourner, who decided to move in to His holy people. Let's actually *believe* that this is true. Let it rise off the pages of your bible. Let it become a reality in your life. God really is in there. Whether you like it or not. Whether you act like it or not. He's in there somewhere. And He's just aching to burst out, in all His richness and glory and abundance and supernaturalness.

Oh, I almost forgot to mention how Paul ends this most excellent chapter of Ephesians.

> *"[The church] is His body, the fullness of Him who fills all in all." (Ephesians 1:23)*

Having been filled to the brim with the Utmost Himself, it's our job to fill everything with Him.

Maybe it's time we got started.

Final Thoughts

I feel it'd be appropriate to close this chapter with the same prayer that Paul prayed for the Church of Ephesus.

Dad, I thank You that each and every day You give me a spirit of wisdom and revelation, so that I would know You more and more. Thank You that You open my eyes, so that I would know what Your amazing plan for my life is. Thank You that You reveal to me who You have made me to be and everything that You have provided for me. And thank You that You continue to show me the power of the Holy Spirit that dwells within me. The same power that raised Christ from the dead is within me. I believe that I am the temple of the Holy Spirit, and I expect for Him to work in my life every day. In Jesus' wonderful name, Amen!

Small Group Questions

1. How does this chapter relate to what you're currently reading in the bible?

2. Do you know that your body is a temple of the Holy Spirit? No really, what are the implications of that statement?

3. What is the difference between God being revealed *to* man, God dwelling *with* man, and God residing *in* man?

4. What is the mystery of the gospel?

5. What are three really big things the power of God is above?

6. What does this mean: "The church is His body, the fullness of Him who fills all in all"?

7. Read Ephesians 1:16-23. What is one notable thing about this verse?

8. What was the main point of this chapter?

7

Great Expectations

Before Cheyne was hired as the fulltime youth pastor at our church, she worked part-time as the youth ministry assistant. Times were rough so to help make ends meet, she also tutored our Pastor's daughter, Katie, for a few hours every week. Katie was in fifth or sixth grade at the time, and on Tuesdays and Thursdays Cheyne would head over to their house to assist Katie with her schoolwork.

On one of those Tuesday afternoon study sessions, Katie was sitting at a cabinet working on her homework when she suddenly let out a distressed cry. Cheyne looked up and headed over to see what was the matter.

"My pencil!" Katie cried, "It fell behind the cabinet!"

Cheyne peered over the back of the cabinet and sure enough, there was a small opening that would perfectly fit a pencil. Cheyne tried to calm Katie down.

"It's not a big deal, Katie, we'll just get a different pencil."

"You don't understand," Katie explained, "that was my *Disney Princess* pencil! I got it at Disneyland!"

Cheyne was already fighting an uphill battle. "Here, let me see if I can get it."

The hole was too small to fit her hand (or anything else for that matter) through it, so Cheyne got on her hands and knees, looking for an opening on the floor. To no avail. She opened the cabinet doors, but that didn't give her access to that impenetrable crevice. In a last ditch effort, she stood to her feet and, putting all the weight she had (which isn't much) into it, she *yanked* on the cabinet. It didn't budge. Not an inch. It seemed to be cemented into the wall. Defeated, she turned to Katie, failure hanging over her shoulders like a bad perm.

"Well... I'm sure you'll go to Disneyland soon. And when you do, you can get a new pencil."

Katie didn't reply.

"Katie?" Cheyne inquired.

Katie had gone back to her homework with a regular pencil, seemingly oblivious to Cheyne's strenuous efforts. She looked up at Cheyne. "Oh, don't worry about it."

"But you were just upset about the pencil."

"Yeah, but it's not a big deal anymore."

Cheyne was confused. "But it was your *Disney Princess* pencil. You got that at Disneyland."

"Yeah, it's okay."

Cheyne was flabbergasted, and Katie caught on, so she offered an explanation.

"When my dad gets home, he'll get it for me."

Cheyne started to get mad.

"What are you talking about? Your dad can't fit his hand in that hole."

Katie shrugged. Cheyne's frustration grew.

"And he won't be able to get access to it through the drawers."

Katie just looked at her. Cheyne's voice got slightly louder.

"And he certainly can't move the cabinet," Cheyne exclaimed. "After all, it's *bolted* to the wall."

Katie was unmoved. Cheyne was now visibly upset.

"So tell me, Katie," Cheyne concluded, "how do you expect your dad to get that pencil?"

Katie looked up at her and smiled. "I don't know."

All reason, all circumstance, all logic indicated that the pencil was lost forever. You can't just detach a cabinet from the wall. Especially to salvage a two dollar pencil. Did Katie expect her dad to punch a hole through the wall? She was being so *unreasonable*. How on earth could her dad get that pencil back? Cheyne had become quite invested in this one-sided argument, so she continued to insist that Katie return to lamenting her lost writing utensil.

"Why aren't you upset anymore?"

Katie started to laugh. "Relax, Cheyne. Here, I'm ready for you to check my math homework."

Grudgingly, Cheyne pulled up a chair and started checking the math problems. Soon, the conversation regarding the prodigal pencil vanished from memory, and after Katie's homework was completed Cheyne headed home. I mistakenly asked how her day was, at which point she filled my ears with the tragic tale of Katie the Unreasonable. And before long, we had eaten dinner, tucked ourselves into bed, and this story faded into a history long since forgotten.

At least, it should have.

But an interesting thing happened two days later. Cheyne pulled up to Pastor's house at three in the afternoon, as she did every Thursday. She walked into the house, put down her purse, and sat down at the table with Katie, as she did every Thursday. Katie looked up, smiled, and pulled out her homework, anxious to begin, as she did every Thursday. And then Cheyne saw it.

Katie's pencil. The *Disney Princess* pencil. The missing pencil, the never-to-be-seen-again pencil. The irretrievable pencil, the "You can't just move a cabinet" pencil. The *impossible* pencil. Right there. In Katie's hand. As if it were nothing. As if it didn't just rise from the dead and walk out of the tomb. Like it was no big deal.

I wasn't there, but from how Katie related the story to me, Cheyne's jaw *literally* dropped to the floor.

"Where'd you get that pencil?" Cheyne asked. Well, more demanded. She didn't ask playfully. She commanded very seriously. Almost fearfully.

"Huh?" Katie was unaware of the miracle that had transpired. Then she saw Cheyne's face, minus one jaw. "Oh. I told you my dad would get it for me."

Cheyne just stood there.

Katie awkwardly tried in vain to engage her in intelligent conversation. "So... should we start?"

And Cheyne never doubted Katie again.

The Impossible

This actually happened. I wasn't there, so I may have taken some creative leaps to fill in the blanks, but ultimately this is a true story. And it's one of my favorite stories. I love this story because it so beautifully illustrates how the seemingly impossible can be so easily achievable.

In 1896, for example, William Thomson, a world-renowned physicist and engineer, refused an invitation to join the Aeronautical Society, claiming he had "not the smallest molecule of faith in aerial navigation other than ballooning." In 1902 he reinforced his opinion, telling an interviewer that "no balloon and no aeroplane will ever be practically successful." It was under two years later that the Wright Brothers took to the skies in the first sustained, controlled, powered, heavier-than-air manned plane, and today, travel by plane is an accepted part of life.

It was also widely believed that the four-minute mile was physically impossible for a sprinter to achieve. And when you look into the past, almost six thousand years of human history had raced by without a sub-four-minute mile. Then came Roger Bannister, who on May 6, 1954 ran a mile in 3 minutes and 59.4 seconds. What a feat, to accomplish something that had been thought undoable! Surely, we would expect years and years and decades and centuries to pass before this achievement was surpassed.

How long did it take?

Forty-six days.

And today, any male runner who wants to be taken serious must be able to run a mile in under 240 seconds.

Why was it so easy for subsequent runners to duplicate this previously unfeasible task? Because they knew it was possible. Roger Bannister took something that had previously been listed under "Impossible, The," and moved it to the other side of the column. He showed that the impossible was attainable.

Einstein denied the existence of black holes. Science, at one point or another, has declared pretty much every possible age of the earth to be impossible. William Thomson, the airplane rejecter, also denied X-rays and the possibility of advancement in physics.

I too once found myself faced with an impossible problem. It was literally titled "The Impossible Problem," and it was given to me by one of my engineering professors in college. Indeed, it seemed unsolvable, and yet I was determined. Professor McNally had presented the problem after a lecture on a Monday, and you should have seen the look on his face when I walked into that lecture hall with four heavily-scribbled sheets of scratch paper in my hands and an ear-to-ear grin on my face.

You see, we as the human race have created an unofficial list, separating what's possible from what's not. It's that list that Roger Bannister disregarded over fifty years ago. One side says "**THE IMPOSSIBLE**" in big bold letters. The other side says "*Sure, It's Possible,*" probably in delicate italicized font. An infinite number of events, questions, desires, and ideas fill in either list, with some topics being placed in the middle. These are those things that seem improbable but have a dynamic following desperately attempting to place them on the latter side. You know, things like "time travel," "Firefly returning," and "the Rolling Stones actually retiring."

It's a nice list, and people don't like it when their lists are messed with. "We have lists for a reason," they might say. "Don't mess with the list."

However, this list has a fundamental flaw. Sure, it's been crafted and reluctantly revised over the years by scientists, politicians, boards and directors. But there is someOne who we never gave the chance to weigh in on the issue. And in my humble opinion, His view is very relevant, seeing as how He majored in the Impossible. And if we would just stop arguing and politicizing and justifying our meager thoughts, we just may be able to see something we missed before.

> *"'For assuredly, I say to you, if you have faith as a mustard seed, you will say to this mountain, "Move from here to there," and it will move; and nothing will be impossible for*

you.'" (Matthew 17:20)

Did Jesus stutter?

Nothing will be impossible for you.

Maybe we should consider throwing that list away.

Shifting the List

What if Christ's church truly believed this was true? Not just words on a page. Not just a hope or wish or fairy tale, but actually true?

Nothing will be impossible for you.

But instead of accepting God at His word, we've developed a habit of using "reason" to explain away any hint of the supernatural: *God doesn't work that way anymore.* We look for excuses that explain why these promises can't possibly come true: *the miraculous was only intended to substantiate the early church.* We pick at these verses until nothing is left, then settle comfortably into obscurity, never knowing the eternal life that Jesus paid for us to have.

When faced with difficulty we (if we turn to God at all) say things like, "What can God do?" You undoubtedly know what I'm talking about. People like to drag out the word "God" when they say it. *What can Gawwwwwd do?* And the implication is, "Nothing, at least not for me." In this we find the vital difference between us and the early church.

We can see this difference so clearly in the tenth chapter of Luke.

In the first half of the chapter, Jesus sends the Seventy out into the world to heal the sick and preach the gospel. Off they go, and some time later they return with joy.

Great Expectations

> *"Then the seventy returned again with joy, saying, 'Lord, even the demons are subject to us in Your name.'"* (Luke 10:17)

Wait a second. Demons have to obey them? I don't remember reading that. Flip back to verse 8, and you'll see that Jesus *only* gave them authority to heal and to preach. Nowhere does Jesus say anything to them about casting out demons. Why on earth would the seventy think that exorcisms were okay?

Right now, someone is reading this and thinking to himself, "Yeah, but *casting out demons* is obviously included in *healing the sick*." Is it that obvious? It wasn't for the disciples. If it were, they wouldn't have returned with joy. They would have returned with apathy, saying, "Lord, the devils are subject to us, just as you said." But they didn't say that. They came back *surprised*.

Picture them out on the mission field. They see a blind guy. Boom! Healed. They see a confused girl. Boom! Preached. A leper. Boom! Healed. Easy enough. Things are going according to plan. They are saying and doing exactly what Jesus instructed them to do. Nothing out of the ordinary (other than healing sick people, of course).

But then they see something they *weren't* expecting: a demon-possessed man. Imagine what was going through their heads.

> *Uh oh! What are we supposed to do? Jesus didn't say anything about demons. Man, are we in trouble. This is impossible.*

But then something happened. One of them had a *crazy* idea. One of them took that unfathomable power of God that had been entrusted to them out of the box. One of them dared to launch out into the deep.

> *Hold on a sec, guys. What* can't *God do?*

This theory caught on like wildfire. These disciples began shifting things on their Impossibilities List.

Yeah, he might be on to something. After all, Jesus could do it.

They began to dream.

Maybe, just maybe, God's power is big enough for that tormented man.

And they dared to trust in God.

What can't God do?

Think of how this scene must've gone down. You have two disciples on the edge of the tightrope getting ready to step forward. But unlike today's disciples, they had made a decision to stop making excuses for why God *wouldn't* show up, and instead *challenged* God to do what only He could do.

Of course, we know how the story ends. They trusted God, stepped out in faith, and lo and behold, it worked! They go running out of town, back to their Teacher. The other disciples heard what happened no doubt, and they too began testing the limits of God's omnipotence. They also discovered the magnificent truth. *There is no limit. Truly, nothing is impossible.* Those two original disciples are joined by two more, and two more, until Jesus looks to the horizon and sees seventy men unabashedly running, dancing, celebrating towards Him.

They finally reach Him, and after taking a few seconds to catch their breaths, one of them manages to squeak out, "Lord, *pant*. The demons, *pant*, they listen to us, *pant*." Jesus then explains this power they wield.

> *"'Behold, I give you the authority to trample on serpents and scorpions, and over all the power of the enemy, and nothing shall by any means hurt you.'"* (Luke 10:19)

My goodness. They had power over all of satan's power. *All of it.* And nothing could hurt them. *Nothing.* Truly, there was nothing they couldn't do. Nothing was impossible to them. And why was that? Because they dared to believe that God was who He said He was.

Unprecedented Things

Of course, religious ideologies are already beginning to creep in, in a vain attempt to persuade you that things are different nowadays and that only a select few could walk in the divine. I once had a conversation with a gentleman ("Jay") who told me that "only Jesus could perform miracles." I took him to Matthew 10, where this power was designated to the twelve disciples.

"Yeah, but it was only for Jesus and the twelve. *Miracles died with the apostles."*

I took him to Luke 10, where the seventy are given the power as well.

"Okay, it's only for the eighty-two."

I mentioned Paul of Tarsus.

"Eighty-three. That's the magic number."

I showed him Luke 9. If you're unfamiliar with the story, the disciples are bickering over which of them is the greatest, a stupid argument that we've all had countless times. Jesus softly reprimands them, telling them that "the least shall be the greatest." On the coat tails of that, John decides to speak up.

> "Now John answered and said, 'Master, we saw someone casting out demons in Your name, and we forbade him because he does not follow with us.'" (Luke 9:49)

Hold the phone. Some *random* guy was casting out demons? This guy wasn't one of the twelve. He wasn't even a part of the seventy. He was just *some guy.* How did some guy manage to demonstrate the power of God? How did this guy bypass the required School of Discipleship that Jesus had only invited His special eighty-two to join? I mean, this guy probably didn't even have a membership badge. How did he walk in the miraculous?

Simple. He stopped making excuses for why God isn't who He is, and started expecting God to show up. He declared *Jesus' name*. And miraculously, it worked!

"What *can't* God do?" And he said it with attitude, emphasizing "can't." The implication: nothing. There is absolutely *nothing* God can't do.

Jay didn't bother with eighty-four.

Sure, we could go through the scriptures and round up every person who ever invoked the power of God. We have these eighty-four, as well as Moses, Elijah, Enoch, Elisha, Abraham, and so on. We could make a tidy little list, with all of the miracle-workers crammed together. Then we could put a fence around them, throw away the key, and agree that the supernatural is unattainable today.

Or, we could dare to dream, just as the disciples did. We could foster obscene notions, like maybe, just maybe, God can do unprecedented things. That God *will* do unprecedented things. We could let the Lion of Judah out of the cage. We could pop open the box, and test the limits of God's promises. We could join the ranks of Orville and Wilbur, Roger Bannister, Katie, and Peter, and venture forth into the impossible.

Abraham was a pretty cool cat. He was one of those visionaries, someone who risked everything he had to step into the unfathomable. He left his family, life, and friends behind when he heard the voice of Yahweh (a God who hadn't been heard from in generations) beckoning him toward a promised land. God delivered. This God then promised him a family, though his wife was barren. Again, God delivered. But then God asked Abraham to trust Him one more time. God asked Abraham to sacrifice his only begotten son, his promised heir.

We read this story and think of it as barbaric. We picture what we would do were we in Abraham's shoes, and when we can't live up to his calling we skip over the passage and hope that none of our unsaved friends ever bring this episode up.

But the bible paints a different picture.

> *"By faith Abraham, when he was tested, offered up Isaac, and he who had received the promises offered up his only begotten son, of whom it was said, 'In Isaac your seed shall be called,' concluding that God was able to raise him up, even from the dead, from which he also received him in a figurative sense."* (Hebrews 11:17-19)

Put yourself in Abraham's position. God gives you a child who is to be the heir of a great nation. However, it seems like your son is going to die. Seemingly contradictory statements. An impossible situation. What do you conclude?

I know what I would conclude. "I misheard God. Isaac is staying right with me. Alive." I'll wager that you feel that way too. Some of you might pretend that you'd be willing to sacrifice your son. "Maybe God will give me another child." After all, all things are possible.

But not Abraham. No, no, no. He knows God's voice. Though they've only spoken a handful of times, Abraham has grown to trust those words which usher forth from his Abba Father. Isaac *will* be my heir. God said it. Therefore, it's true.

Problem is, Isaac can't be dead *and* my heir. After all, God is the God of the living (Mark 12:26-27). It's got to be one or the other. Will Isaac live, or will he die?

Then Abraham comes to a conclusion. A crazy conclusion. A beautifully crazy off-his-rockers conclusion. He concludes that *both* will be true. Isaac will die, but he will also live. After all, that's what God said. And if God said it, it *must* be true (oh, how I wish there were more Christians who thought thus).

Abraham steps into the impossible.

> *"Concluding that God was able to raise him up, even from the dead."* (Hebrews 11:19)

Now let me interrupt the narrative right here. As you read this, you probably don't think that this outrageous conclusion is that far-fetched. After all, Elijah raised people from the dead. And Jesus raised people from the dead. Then Jesus *was* raised from the dead. Paul raised people from the dead. Heck, you and I have been raised from the dead. The bible tells us all of these things. The idea that God could raise someone from the dead isn't that extreme (or at least it shouldn't be).

But for Abraham, none of those miracles had taken place yet. Elijah and Jesus and Paul weren't born yet. Not only that, but the book of Genesis wasn't even written yet (how could it have been? Abraham is the main character). Abraham didn't have *any* examples of the dead being raised. He didn't even have any promises of the dead being raised. This notion of resurrection came completely out of left field.

This expectation from God was unprecedented. God had *never* done anything like that before. But when Abraham decided to believe that the impossible was easy for God, I bet a huge smile crept over God's face. I bet the angels rejoiced. I bet Jesus gave the Holy Spirit a high-five. And I bet the archangel Michael started moon-walking down those streets made of gold.

Abraham believed in the impossible. No wonder he is cited as our prime example of faith. No wonder he is the father of our many nations. No wonder God choose him to exemplify His legacy here on the earth.

> *"He did not waver at the promise of God through unbelief, but was strengthened in faith, giving glory to God, and being fully convinced that what He had promised He was also able to perform."* (Romans 4:20-21)

Read my lips. *Nothing. Is. Impossible.* Nothing. Absolutely nothing. No, there is not one thing that isn't possible. As Audrey Hepburn famously pointed out, "The word itself says *I'm possible.*" But then that begs the question: Why do we have that word in our vernacular? If there is nothing that is impossible, is there even a need for that word? Our previously discussed List should be empty on the "Impossible" side. I scoff at anything someone attempts to put over there.

In fact, I have had my fair share of "Impossible" events take place. Some are big, but I tend to like the small ones more. Yes, I find it over-the-top spectacular that God wants to heal the woman stricken with cancer, but when God cares enough to help with the small details of your life as well, that's pretty exciting.

Several Christmases ago, in an attempt to save money, Cheyne and I "made" gifts for our family members. My dad was to receive a mixed CD, cleverly titled "Feliz NaviDAD." I made the playlist on iTunes, but when I went to burn the disc, an error message popped up. The CD drive was broken.

I had a couple of days to make the CD and I resolved to do it at work, but in the holiday rush it was overlooked, and suddenly Christmas was upon us, the CD was non-existent, and my parents were on their way over. I was in trouble. I had wasted time, I had been careless, I had dropped the ball, and now there was no hope.

But then I stopped making excuses, and let God out of the cage. *What can't God do?*

I prayed. I declared that since God makes all thing *work for good* when you pray in the spirit (Romans 8:26-28), He can probably also make all things *work good* when you pray in the spirit. My computer wasn't working *good*, so I prayed that it would begin to work *good*. Yes, it was a stretch, and yes, it was grammatically incorrect, but for whatever crazy reason I had this notion that God would take care of business.

And took care of business He did. He showed up. My computer began to work good. After all, God *is* good. So it logically follows that good things will happen when God gets involved. By the time my parents arrived on that sunny Christmas morning, the CD was burned and personally hand-labeled. And my dad listens to that CD to this day.

Several weeks later we invited a couple of friends over to watch a movie. As they were pulling up, my DVD player stopped working. I restarted it. I cleaned off the disc. I tapped on the side of the machine. But still, it wouldn't work.

I wasn't even fazed. "God, You said that all things would work for good to those who love You, and I love You. And if You can make things work *for* good, You can certainly make my DVD player work good, just like You did with my computer. Thank You that my DVD player works, in the name of Jesus!" Then I laid hands on the contraption and prayed in the spirit for five minutes.

Need I tell you how that night ended? Alas, we all enjoyed the movie.

Probably a year later I was working at our church office when the secretary came in. "My car won't start. Can anyone here help me?"

Almost reflexively I was on my feet, walking towards her car. Suddenly, a million thoughts were racing through my head. "You don't know anything about cars." And that was true. I still don't know anything about cars. "You've never fixed a car." "What on earth are you thinking?"

But then I remembered God's faithfulness. So I prayed. Just as I had before. And when I reached the car, I simply laid hands on it and asked her to start the car. That puppy revved up like nobody's business.

"Oh, I guess it wasn't broken after all," she said. But I knew the truth. In addition to being the Great Physician, my God is also apparently the Great Mechanic.

I am confident that there is nothing that is impossible for me. Absolutely nothing.

Well, actually, that's not entirely true. There is *one* thing.

> "But without faith it is impossible to please Him, for he who comes to God must believe that He is, and that He is a rewarder of those who diligently seek Him." (Hebrews 11:6)

Only one thing is impossible. And that one thing is to please God without faith. To deny that God can do anything. To deny that God *will* do anything. But if we step out of our comfort zone, if we dare to dream, if we venture out into the land of impossibilities and absurdities and faith, God will always show up. Time and time again, He has proven Himself faithful. And luckily for us, He will never change.

> *Alice laughed: "There's no use trying," she said; "one can't believe impossible things."*
>
> *"I daresay you haven't had much practice," said the Queen. "When I was younger, I always did it for half an hour a day. Why, sometimes I've believed as many as six impossible things before breakfast." (Alice in Wonderland)*

Final Thoughts

Concerning the limits of our faith, Jesus said, "You will have whatever you say" (Mark 11:23). Truly, nothing is impossible for the child of God. Whatever is going on in your life, whatever you need, go to your loving Dad in prayer, completely confident in His ability and desire to answer your prayers, and you will receive.

Dad, You said nothing is impossible for him that believes. I believe that what You've said is true. And because it's true, I am confident that I will receive whatever I need in the name of Jesus. Whether it's something big like healing and provision, or something small like fixing my DVD player, nothing is impossible for You. Thank You that you continue to do impossible things in my life every single day!

Small Group Questions

1. How does this chapter relate to what you're currently reading in the bible?

2. What are some things that were once thought to be impossible that have since been achieved?

3. What are some impossible things that took place in the bible?

4. What are some impossible things that have taken place in your life (or the life of someone you know)?

5. What gave Abraham the crazy idea that God could raise Isaac from the dead?

6. Is there anything that God can't do? Is there anything that you can't do?

7. Read Luke 10:17-19. What is one notable thing about this verse?

8. What was the main point of this chapter?

8
Greater Expectations

Peter was a pretty cool guy. Sure, he talked way too much (which I can relate to) and often acted irrationally (which I can relate to as well), but the man was absolutely in love with Jesus. Whatever Jesus was talking about or doing, everyone knew Peter would be right by His side. He was one of the few disciples who made up Jesus' "Inner Circle," gaining him access to such special events as the healing of Jairus' daughter, the transfiguration (where he sort of met Moses and Elijah), and Jesus' final prayer sesh in the Garden of Gethsemane. He is also the only disciple who was both complimented for hearing from God and insulted for acting like satan in the same paragraph (Matthew 16:13-23).

And I have to laugh whenever I read Peter's contributions at the Last Supper (John 13). Jesus says to His followers, "I'm going to wash your feet now."

Peter will have *none* of that! "You shall never wash my feet!" he staunchly declares.

Jesus levels with him. "If I do not wash your feet, you will have no part with Me."

Peter realizes his error, and not wanting to lose his close relationship with Jesus, quickly begins backpedalling. "Don't stop at my feet, Jesus. Wash everything!" Peter figures if washing his feet is good, then washing the rest of him will be even better. "My hands, my head, all of me! Wash on, Lord!"

Jesus just stares at him awkwardly for a couple of seconds, which probably seemed like an eternity to Peter. "Yeah… I'm just going to wash your feet. That'll be enough."

Finally Peter takes the hint and stops talking.

Man, I love that guy! I'm looking forward to meeting him someday. You just have to respect a man that was willing to go all in for Jesus. He definitely had his fair share of blunders, but he was always the first one to volunteer for Jesus' wacky schemes, and that's a great thing to have on your résumé.

One such scheme was on the stormy waters of the Sea of Galilee. The disciples are sailing across the sea in the middle of the night, planning to meet Jesus on the other side the following morning. Suddenly, one of them spots a ghost hovering towards them across the open waters. Terror grips them. *A ghost!* They make like Scooby Doo for the dark recesses of the ship, hoping that the apparition won't notice them.

But then, they hear the familiar voice of Jesus, calling out from the waves, "It's me, guys. Don't be afraid." (Matthew 14:27) The disciples are still horrified, but Peter stops cowering long enough to hatch a crazy idea: "If it's really you, Jesus, command me to walk out there with you!" (Verse 28)

This is absolutely bonkers. For one, if it's *not* Jesus then Peter is as good as dead. He'll be continuously pummeled by the freezing waves of this Galilean lake at four o'clock in the morning, surrounded by complete darkness. *And* there'll be an angry ghost out there with him. He'd never survive the night. But this idea is also crazy for a second, more scriptural reason. Peter, as well as Jesus and the other disciples, would have grown up reading the Old Testament (or as they called it, *The* Testament). And they were no doubt familiar with a certain passage from the book of Job.

> "[God] alone spreads out the heavens, and treads on the waves of the sea." (Job 9:8)

Can you believe Peter's gall? Oh the nerve! What a pompous, arrogant fool! Only God can walk on water. How dare Peter try to steal the power which is reserved for God alone. Certainly Jesus won't tolerate this blasphemy. Certainly He will reprimand Peter, commanding him to "stay in the boat, satan." Surely Jesus will show Peter the error of his ways and set him on the right path.

He sets Peter on a path, alright.

"So Jesus said, 'Come.' And when Peter had come down out of the boat, he walked on the water to go to Jesus." (Matthew 14:29)

Hold on. We must have missed something. The bible clearly states that *God alone* can walk on water. And yet it sounds like Jesus just invited Peter to walk alongside of Him. That cannot be right. Maybe Jesus was unfamiliar with the book of Job. Maybe He had only read the first two and last two chapters of Job, like the rest of us. Maybe He simply *didn't know* that walking on water was only for the Divine.

Okay, that's probably unlikely. Jesus must've known what the Word said. After all, He *is* the Word. If anyone would know, He would.

So what gives? Why would Jesus lead Peter out onto those stormy waves? Why would Jesus allow – no, encourage – Peter to do something so seemingly unscriptural? Why would Jesus call Peter to participate in something so clearly reserved for God, and God alone?

Walk on Water

The magnitude of this event, this triumph over the laws of gravity, is an event that the church has overlooked for far too long. Usually, all we glean from this is that Jesus was Lord over Nature before quickly moving on to the next chapter. Sometimes we make a connection about keeping our eyes fixed upon Christ rather than the circumstances that surround us. Maybe we'll even say something about faith. But that's usually the end of the discussion. Then it's on to another head-to-head showdown with the Pharisees.

But see the extravagant procession that occurs here. Peter isn't just stepping out of a boat and onto the waves. He's stepping out of mankind and into the heavenly. In this passage we see Jesus inviting Peter to walk in the divine. Actually, that's not exactly how it happened. Peter *asks* for permission to step into the divine, and Jesus answers with a resolute "yes."

Think of how most biblical scholars and post-modern pastors would have responded if they had been sailing in that ship. After building up the courage to face the ghost, many an insult would be flying over those waters.

> *"How dare you demand of God!"*

> *"What pride! To assume that you could live like God!"*

> *"Doesn't Peter know that the supernatural has ceased?"*

Followed by eloquent self-degradation in the guise of humility.

Yet Jesus doesn't reprimand Peter. He beckons Him. I would bet that Jesus' heart was filled with joy upon hearing Peter's request. I wonder if Jesus saw it coming or not. I'm sure none of the disciples could have predicted what Peter would say.

> *"Command me to come to You on the water."*

Jesus obliged, Peter stepped down, and the laws of physics bowed at Peter's feet. But the victory was short-lived, for the boisterous waves caught Peter's attention and fear took over. He began to sink (how does one *begin* to sink?) and cried out for help. In the blink of an eye, Jesus is there, pulling him from the depths and carrying him into the safety of the boat.

This would have been a perfect time for Jesus to explain,

> *"You know, Peter, I'm glad we got to share this special moment together, but walking on water is just for Me, Pops, and the Holy Spirit. That's why you sunk."*

Or maybe something a bit more King-James-esque.

> *"O thou sinful man of measly humanity, thy canst not expect*

to be likened unto Me."

But Jesus doesn't chalk this slip-up off to Peter's humanity. Nor does He claim it as a special occasion ended by Sovereignty.

> *"Immediately Jesus stretched out His hand and caught him, and said to him, 'O you of little faith, why did you doubt?'"* (Matthew 14:31)

Jesus places responsibility for Peter's brief success and eventual failure squarely on *Peter*. It was *Peter's* faith that allowed him to walk on water. And it was *Peter's* doubt that caused him to sink. In fact, Jesus implied that Peter should have been able to continue on his amphibious stroll with Jesus. You can sense a hint of a smile in Jesus' response. "Why did you doubt, Peter? I've been waiting for one of you guys to rise to the challenge for months! And you were so close!"

This event must have had a profound impact on Peter. This experience, this invitation to live like God, characterized his ministry through the book of Acts. His boldness is tangible as he preaches to three thousand traveling Jews on Pentecost. His audacity as he pulls the crippled beggar to his feet at the Gate called Beautiful is inspiring. This guy had received a taste of heaven and from then on he was hooked. He couldn't get enough.

But what about you and me? Surely Peter was special. He was one of the twelve, after all. And really, one of the three that made up Jesus' inner circle. You and I couldn't possibly hope to step into the divine like he did. Or could we?

> *"As His divine power has given to us all things that pertain to life and godliness, through the knowledge of Him who called us by glory and virtue, by which have been given to us exceedingly great and precious promises, that through these you may be partakers of the divine nature, having escaped the corruption that is in the world through lust."* (2 Peter 1:3-4)

I wonder if Peter was reminiscing about that spectacular stormy night when he wrote these beautiful words.

God has already provided everything necessary for life (the Greek *zoe*, literally meaning "the absolute fullness of life which belongs to God") and godliness. Understand that. God has given you *His* life. For God so loved the world that He gave His only begotten Son, that we would have *His* life. The thief came to destroy, but Jesus came that we would live in the fullness of *His* life. That is the life that God gives us. Not simply a resuscitated heartbeat, but the very life of Yahweh Himself. And as we embrace this godly life that Christ wants us to live, that Christ *died* for us to live, we are invited to become partners in the nature of God Himself. We are invited to step out into the impossible. We are invited to walk on water.

Greater Works Than These

The notion of living a supernatural lifestyle like Jesus is simply breathtaking to me. I mean, think of all the awesome things Jesus did. First off, He walked on top of water. That's pretty impressive. But there's more. A lot more.

He turned water into wine. He calmed raging seas on more than one occasion. He opened blind eyes. He dished out expert fishing advice. He healed multitudes. He fed thousands upon thousands of strangers with a kindergartener's sack lunch. He cast out demons. He drained a tree of its life overnight. He pulled money out of fish. He saw the future. He raised the dead.

And He gave that authority over to you and me.

How does one even respond to that notion? I can do what Jesus did. That's pretty cool. I mean, when your only limitation is what Jesus was able to do, I feel it's safe to say you've got it made. But then Jesus takes things a step further.

> *"'Most assuredly, I say to you, he who believes in Me, the works that I do he will do also; and greater works than these he will do, because I go to My Father.'" (John 14:12)*

Excuse me?

"You will do greater works."

What does that even mean? *Greater works*? What the heck is a greater work? Look at Jesus' portfolio. He cured diseases that had haunted people for decades. He fed over ten thousand people with practically nothing. Twice. He had power over trees. He had power over water. He had power over animals. He had power over food. He had power over weather. He had power over everything physical. He had power over everything spiritual. He did it all. The Man even stopped *dying*. What is greater than that? What could possibly qualify as a so-called "greater work"?

Maybe when Jesus said we would do greater works, He didn't mean *quality*. He must've meant *quantity*. Yeah, that must be it. I'll do *more* works than Jesus. That shouldn't be too tough. After all, He was only doing miracles for three and a half years, and I'm going to be around for at least another seventy years or so. I have plenty of time to do *more* works than Jesus.

> *"And there are also many other things that Jesus did, which if they were written one by one, I suppose that even the world itself could not contain the books that would be written. Amen." (John 21:25)*

Wow.

To give you some perspective, the Library of Congress is the world's largest library. Now, this isn't your typical elementary school library. The place takes up more than four entire buildings in Washington, D.C., and is staffed by over 3,500 people. There are over 151 million items stored there, 22,765,967 of which are catalogued books. An average book contains approximately 100,000 words. This means that the Library of Congress contains at least *two trillion* printed words. The gospels contain 86,731.

That tells me that Jesus did a *ton* of awesome things that I don't even know about! When I read the gospels, I'm not getting a detailed description of every single work Jesus ever did. The gospels really only account for about seventeen days of Jesus' life. I'm getting a smorgasbord of miracles meant to give me a small glimpse into the days of Jesus. The gospels aren't supposed to be an exhaustive list of events; no, it's only an ever-so-brief retelling of a few very important details. And what can we expect? After all, if God tried to give us a full account of Jesus' life, no one would have ever reached the book of Acts yet! We'd still be stuck in the 497th chapter of Matthew.

All that to say, *greater works* can't mean *more works*. The sheer magnitude of things that Jesus did trumps every bookstore, library, and university in North America. So what can this verse possibly mean? Greater works isn't more works; it's also not better works. What on earth was Jesus trying to tell us?

Sorry to break it to you, but I don't know. I'm not sure if you were expecting an answer, but if so you're not going to get one from me. This is a mystery, as far as I'm concerned. My finite mind can't comprehend what a "greater work" would be. And yet, my spirit is stirred up inside of my very being to go out and *do* these incomprehensible greater works. You see, I don't know what a "greater work" is, but I do know one thing. I can do them. I can do these unknown greater works. Jesus said I could.

Not only did Jesus say that I *could* do works greater than His, He took it a step further. He said I *would* do them.

*"Greater works than these he **will** do…" (John 14:12)*

We are supposed to do greater works. No longer is this a fantastical theory. No longer is this a thrilling possibility to be discussed at length in coffee shops and churches and bible studies. This is a command, an order, a decree from the mouth of our Lord and King. *Do greater works.* We aren't commanded to sit around and talk about what these verses mean. We're not told to argue about the implications of these grandeur promises. We're not even told to post these quotes on facebook and hope for a dozen or so "likes." We're told to *do*.

And herein lies a fundamental difference between the Western World and the Eastern World. Here in the West we fancy ourselves as philosophers. We think. We deduce. We figure stuff out. And we end up with textbooks of theory, theory that will never be practiced. But the early church didn't *talk*. They *did*. They wouldn't've asked, "What does this scripture mean to you?" They'd say, "How are you *doing* this scripture?" or "How does this scripture work in your life?" They weren't a people of *knowing*. They were a people of *doing*. And if you weren't doing, no one cared what you knew. If it didn't translate into action, it didn't matter.

It's so easy to miss this when reading through the scriptures with our Western mentality, but if you pay close attention, the bible is saturated with this concept. Look at how Jesus often ended His sermons.

> *"Then Jesus said to him, 'Go and **do** likewise.'"* (Luke 10:37)

> *"'Therefore whoever hears these sayings of Mine, and **does** them, I will liken him to a wise man who built his house on the rock.'"* (Matthew 7:24)

> *"'For whoever **does** the will of My Father in heaven is My brother and My sister and mother.'"* (Mark 3:35)

> *"'But he who received seed on the good ground is he who hears the word and understands it, who indeed **bears fruit** and **produces**.'"* (Matthew 13:23)

> *"And He said to him, 'You have answered rightly; **do** this and you will live.'"* (Luke 10:28)

> *"'More than that, blessed are those who hear the word of God and **keep** it!'"* (Luke 11:28)

> "'You are My friends if you **do** whatever I command you.'" (John 15:14)
>
> "'If you know these things, blessed are you if you **do** them.'" (John 13:17)
>
> "'Blessed is that servant whom his master will find so **doing** when he comes.'" (Luke 12:43)
>
> "'But why do you call Me "Lord, Lord," and not **do** the things which I say?'" (Luke 6:46)
>
> "'If you love Me, **keep** My commandments.'" (John 14:15)

This isn't some fairy tale or pipe dream. Jesus meant what He said. *Do greater works.* And if Jesus commanded you to do greater works, that means it's *possible* for you to do greater works. You can *expect* greater works. Open yourself up to this absolute truth. Allow the Word of God to break through all of those preconceived notions of your own unworthiness. Accept God at His word. Believe. *You can do greater works.*

Plugged In

What is it that enables us to do greater works? What turned that dream into a reality?

> "'Most assuredly, I say to you, he who believes in Me, the works that I do he will do also; and greater works than these he will do, because I go to My Father.'" (John 14:12)

Did you catch it?

> "'Because I go to My Father.'"

Jesus leaving planet earth makes greater works possible.

That seems pretty counter-intuitive. After all, Jesus was the one who started the works in the first place. Does it really make sense that Him leaving would cause the works to increase?

Most Christians very much desire that Jesus was still here. I heard a disheartening sermon from a traveling minister several years ago about this very topic. She was lamenting the fact that God is sometimes unfair, and her primary example was that God took Jesus away from us. And then she sighed and, concluding her argument, said, "I mean, I guess we have the Holy Spirit, so that's okay."

Having the Holy Spirit is just okay?

Listen to the words Jesus used to describe the Holy Spirit.

> *"'Nevertheless I tell you the truth. It is to your advantage that I go away; for if I do not go away, the Helper will not come to you; but if I depart, I will send Him to you.'" (John 16:7)*

Jesus viewed the Holy Spirit's entrance into the world as a extraordinary event. Something to look forward to. Something to be desired. He said that having the Holy Spirit here on the earth was *better* than having Jesus Himself. With Jesus present upon the earth the church could do "the works that He did," but with the Holy Spirit present the church could venture out of the boat into the "greater works than these."

Does this mean that the Holy Spirit is greater than Jesus? Absolutely not! Neither the Father nor the Son nor the Spirit is any greater than the others. They are all co-equal and co-awesome. But they have different roles to play in your life. This becomes evident when you study how Jesus spoke about the Holy Spirit.

You may be familiar with the Greek word *Parakletos*. This is the word Jesus used to describe the Holy Spirit. It can be translated several ways, the most common being *Comforter, Counselor, Helper, Intercessor, Advocate, Strengthener,* and *Standby*. That is the role that the Holy Spirit plays in our lives. Jesus described the Holy Spirit with this word four times, and all four times He specifically said that the *Comforter* was sent to abide with you forever (John 14:16,

26; John 15:26; John 16:7). And yet this word *Parakletos* is used a fifth time in the scriptures, though it doesn't refer to the Holy Spirit this final time.

> *"My little children, these things I write to you, so that you may not sin. And if anyone sins, we have an* **Advocate** *with the Father, Jesus Christ the righteous."* (1 John 2:1)

Jesus Christ is also our *Parakletos*. That makes sense. I mean, Jesus did say that He was sending us *another* One. That implies that He was the first One. We have two *Parakletos*. And the main difference between them is their current position. The Holy Spirit is with us, while Jesus is "with the Father."

Have you seen *Back to the Future*? In the final moments of the film, Marty McFly is barreling his DeLorean down the streets of Hill Valley toward the clock tower, which Doc Brown has conveniently hooked up to an intricate array of wires. Their plan: when the lightning strikes the tower, the electricity will shoot through the wires and into Marty's passing car, zapping him back to 1985.

But trouble strikes. A bolt of lightning crashes into a nearby tree, causing a branch to fall onto Doc's elaborate system of wires. The cable at the clock tower becomes unplugged, dashing all hope of Marty's return to the future.

Doc Brown must act fast. He bolts up the spiraling staircase to the pinnacle of the tower, grabs the loose cable, and plugs it back in. Unfortunately, this causes the plug at the *bottom* of the tower to become unplugged.

Every time I watch this scene I think to myself, *If only there were two of them. One at the top and one at the bottom. Then the problem would be solved.* Well guess what? You've got two *Parakletos*. You've got one at the top, and you've got one down here. And Their job is to keep you plugged into heaven. That's why Jesus said it was necessary for Him to leave. He had to plug us in.

This gives a whole new understanding to Jesus' final command to the church before His ascension.

> *"'Behold, I send the Promise of My Father upon you; but tarry in the city of Jerusalem until you are endued with power from on high.'" (Luke 24:49)*

Jesus told them to wait until the Spirit came. Why? Because having us plugged in up top wouldn't do us any good if we weren't connected down here, too. But the Holy Spirit did come, and as promised, the church received the power necessary to transform the world.

The Holy Spirit is absolutely vital to your success on the earth. We cannot hope to live in the power, the authority, the *life* that God meant for us to have if we don't appreciate the Spirit's never-failing presence in our lives. The church has been infamous for overlooking this precious gift from God, and yet we read that it is the Holy Spirit who is the key to Christian living.

> *"Now He who establishes us with you in Christ and has anointed us is God, who also has sealed us and given us the Spirit in our hearts as a guarantee." (2 Corinthians 1:21-22)*

The proof that you are forever linked to heaven is the Holy Spirit, who has been given to you. The Spirit isn't some consolation prize that Jesus sent to help us get over Him. The Holy Spirit is our lifeline! And without Him, we can do nothing. We've seen this proven out, as many parishioners have tried in vain to live without the indwelling power of the Holy Spirit, and have ended up accomplishing nothing.

Jesus paid the price for the greater works He commanded you to do, but the Spirit was sent to make those dreams a reality. You have a hand-signed guarantee from God that you can do greater works. His name is the Holy Spirit.

Exceedingly Abundant

There is a final scripture that will conclude this chapter rather nicely.

> *"Now to Him who is able to do exceedingly abundantly above all that we ask or think, according to the power that works in us." (Ephesians 3:20)*

I love this because it brings the focus back to God. *He* is able to do these greater works. Sure, I'm the vessel, but I'm sure not the source. I'm not rich on my own; I'm simply plugged into my Daddy.

And when I allow God to work through me, look what is accomplished. God does all that I ask or think. *All* of it. But not only does God do all of it. He does *above* all of it. But that's still not enough for God. He does *abundantly* above all of it. And why stop there? God does *exceedingly* abundantly above all of it.

And where has God placed that power? Where is that magnificent treasure hidden?

In us.

That's mind boggling. His treasure has been tucked away in these earthen vessels. And it's just waiting to pour out of us.

So we are faced with a decision here. Just as Peter timidly stood inside the relative safety of his boat, so we are here in the relative safety of our comfort zones and preconceived notions. But Christ is standing out in the deep, calling to us. Inviting us. Beckoning to us.

Step out of the boat, and into the divine.

Do you trust Him?

Final Thoughts

To end this chapter, I have a prayer and a challenge for you:

God, Your Word says that I would do the same works that Jesus did, and even greater works than those. And because the unfathomable power of the Holy Spirit flows through my veins, I thank You that this is a reality in my life. I will do greater works, because I am plugged into You. Send me, Dad, out into this dying world to reach the lost. Call me, Jesus, to step out of the boat and walk upon the waves. Lead me, Holy Spirit, to do impossible things, to do great works and mighty miracles. I am not afraid. I trust in You. And I will follow wherever You lead me.

Now here is the challenge: Go do those greater works. Stop questioning God's ability, and just *do* it. Jump on in. The water's rather nice today.

Small Group Questions

1. How does this chapter relate to what you're currently reading in the bible?

2. How was Peter able to walk on water, when Job 9:8 seemingly said he couldn't? What caused Peter to sink?

3. Why did Jesus ascend into heaven?

4. What does the word *parakletos* mean?

5. What is the most impressive miracle you can think of that was performed by someone other than Jesus? Do you have the same power?

6. Can you do the same works Jesus did? Why?

7. Read John 14:12-14. What is one notable thing about this verse?

8. What was the main point of this chapter?

9
Worthy

Just under a month ago my wife and I moved.

For those of you who have relocated recently, I'm fairly certain you just shuddered as you read that sentence. Moving, for those of you that have never done it (or have since blocked those vile memories from your mind), is a horrible ordeal. You have all sorts of useless garbage all over the place that you don't want and certainly don't need, but for whatever absurd reason you can't seem to part with it. My *Terminator* poster, for instance, or that stop-sign my brother-in-law gave me for Christmas (which I sure hope he came across in a legal manner). If you finally manage to build up the strength and courage to get rid of those precious items, your spouse will inevitably find them in the "donations" box and, thinking you had a temporary lapse in judgment, move them into the "Garrett's Stuff" box.

To all of the married men out there, your wife probably has hundreds of tree branches, leaves, logs, flowers, and other natural "treasures" that she has collected over the years from various hikes, picnics, and camping trips, which she assures you will one day be used in a DIY (male translation: Do It Yourself) project of biblical proportions that will soon grace the pages of *Pinterest*. My wife had a stockpile of it in our garage. And it all had to be pristinely packed as well. You wouldn't know it, but it takes a lot of bubble wrap to save the junk you find on the ground in the woods.

We didn't have enough room in our new place for everything in the moving trucks. We didn't have enough trucks for all of the boxes. We didn't have enough boxes for all of our stuff. And yet, for some inescapable reason, we still thought we didn't have enough stuff. It's one of the many paradoxes of life.

A week before we moved, a friend of ours claimed that if she had to move again she would just sell all of her belongings along with the house and buy new furniture for the new place. We laughed, thinking it was merely a joke, but after having moved we understand perfectly. It was no joke.

And we were actually quite fortunate throughout this whole process. We had over a dozen friends come over to help during the course of a week, friends who packed, lifted, stacked, moved, sorted, strapped down, and unloaded for hours on end. Our friends are pretty awesome.

But with all of this help, we still only barely managed to get out of the house on time. We needed to be out by Thursday night, and on Wednesday afternoon, after almost five days of constant packing, we still felt like we had hardly made a dent. In fact, I know that we wouldn't've made it out on time if not for the very gracious help of a friend.

At around four o'clock on Wednesday afternoon I was standing in the middle of our storage unit, drenched in sweat and surrounded by an elaborate mountain range of cardboard boxes, metal bed frames, wooden dining chairs, and a particularly heavy armoire, when I received a text message.

> How much stuff do you have left to move

I responded.

> About a garage worth

Ten minutes passed. Then this.

> We are getting you guys movers

> They'll come out tomorrow and finish

> It's already in motion

Flabbergasted. That's really the only word that can appropriately describe the feeling that I felt at that moment. I felt like a huge weight had been lifted from my shoulders. Literally. There was a weighty file cabinet I had been balancing between my shoulder blades, which I now felt free to let slide to the floor. I sat down on my makeshift chair (which in reality was three-fourths of a Yamaha mini-bike), wiped the dirt and grime and sweat and packing tape from my brow, and let out a huge sigh of relief.

Utterly flabbergasted. I mean, I had done absolutely nothing to deserve this sort of unwarranted generosity. I hadn't tutored his kids or purchased a really great birthday present for him. This kindness he had shown for my family was completely uncalled for. And yet it was so.

The next day, the movers showed up at 8:30 a.m. as promised. And a peculiar thing happened, or rather didn't happen: not one of the movers told me how undeserving I was of their services. None of them sat me down to explain that I had not earned their labor. Not even the owner of the moving company felt compelled to come out and tell me that this favor my friend had bestowed upon me was unmerited. Not one of them said a word.

Why?

Because the price had already been paid. Whether I was worthy of this compassionate gift or not, it was mine. And you had better believe I took advantage of it.

Defining Grace

I remember visiting a friend's youth service many years ago. My wife had just been hired as the full-time youth pastor at our church, and as excited as we were, we also knew we didn't have a clue how to run a youth group. So the following Wednesday we headed over to the church where our friend Jim was youth pastoring, and after their service ended we sat down on their plush couches to talk ministry. The students slowly filtered out of the youth building as their parents picked them up, but we remained for hours and hours, soaking up wisdom and coffee until well after midnight. Eventually the caffeine wore off and we said our goodbyes, loaded up into the car, and headed home, slightly more prepared for the adventure that lay ahead of us.

Jim is a really great guy, and he gave us lots of great advice that evening, but there is one thing I remember above everything else he said that night. He was telling us the importance of simplifying topics, so the kids could better learn them. Then he gave this as an example.

> "We use a lot of mnemonic devices around here. For example, 'Grace' is '**G**od's **R**iches **A**t **C**hrist's **E**xpense.'"

And as embarrassed as I am to admit it, that was the first time I ever understood what grace was.

Don't get me wrong. Before that evening, I *knew* what grace was. Sort of. I mean, I had a vague concept somewhere out in the far reaches of my mind. If someone had asked me if I knew what grace was, I would have immediately responded, "Yes!" But if someone had asked me *what* grace was, I would have awkwardly dodged the question until they lost interest and walked away. And sadly, I think that's how most Christians feel about grace. They kind of know what it is, but they don't actually *know* what it is. And the church, by and large, hasn't really done a great job of giving a cohesive definition of grace. Not until recently.

There is a common definition of grace going around nowadays. You've probably heard it before. *Unmerited favor.* Unfortunately, this definition often gives people the wrong idea about grace, about God, and about themselves. You see, the problem with this definition is the word "unmerited." It is laced with the notorious *unworthiness complex*, which burrowed itself deep under the skin of Christ's church centuries ago and has remained hidden ever since. And it is this feeling of unworthiness that has become a major hindrance to successful Christian living. We ask God to give us strength on our way to work, but we feel unworthy of His favor. The devil immediately picks up on that, assuring us that we are indeed unworthy of anything we ask of God. We begin to lose confidence that our prayer will even be heard, much less answered, and as a result we don't receive. Was the problem God's willingness to answer our prayer? Of course not! It was our lack of confidence in the God who desires to answer our prayers. This problem is rooted in this cloak of unworthiness that Christians love to throw over their shoulders. And that simply isn't the kind of baggage a Christian needs to be carrying around with them every day.

Now, some of you are reading this and thinking to yourselves, "But we are unworthy." And that could not be further from the truth. Here's why.

Imagine that someone at your church walked up to you, and for no reason handed you a crisp one hundred dollar bill, fresh from the US Treasury. Did you earn that money? Of course not. But is it yours? Absolutely. And since it belongs to you, you now have a legal right to that money, and everything that can be purchased with it.

How silly would it be if the bank refused to deposit that money into your checking account because they didn't feel you deserved it? Or if Wal-Mart wouldn't sell you the latest special edition Blu-Ray release of *The Dark Knight Rises* because you didn't work hard enough for that money? That'd be ludicrous! Whether the gift was merited or not became completely irrelevant the moment you received it. It's yours now. And that's all that matters.

Still, many Christians live under this notion that they are unworthy of everything God wants to give them. But here's a question: can you be unworthy of something if God felt compelled to give it to you?

Let me be clear, lest I be misunderstood. I'm not saying that we did anything to earn salvation, grace, or divine love. What I am saying is that when God freely saved you, He made you into someone who was worthy of His blessings.

I think it'll add credence to my claims if we consider how the word "unworthy" is used in the scriptures. This word appears four times in the New Testament, and *every single time* Paul is reprimanding Christians for thinking they are unworthy. Paul's commentary on unworthiness is pretty straightforward: *You're not unworthy, so quit acting like it*!

Here's the bottom line. I didn't deserve anything that God has so graciously given to me. I was an enemy of God, trapped in sin and an all-around not-good guy. But God plucked me up out of the miry clay, cleaned me off, and adopted me into His awesome family. As a sinner, I deserved nothing. Absolutely nothing. But praise God that I'm not a sinner any longer. No, I am God's kid now. And as the cherished son of my Dad, I am worthy of His blessings. I am worthy of His favor. I am worthy of His love.

Why?

Jesus' blood has made me worthy.

Sozo-Salvation

So where does that leave us? We've lost *unmerited*. All that we're left with is *favor*. And don't get me wrong, favor is awesome. Just as the saints of old, we have found favor in God's sight. But grace is a lot more than just favor. Let's look at what the bible says about grace.

> "For by grace you have been saved through faith, and that not of yourselves; it is the gift of God." (Ephesians 2:8)

Grace saves. But from what, exactly? Christians colloquially refer to themselves as "saved," but do we ever stop to ask what we are saved from? After all, Lois Lane might consider herself saved when she's held in the arms of Superman. Children rescued from a burning building are also saved. As Christians, it's important to recognize not just that we're "saved," but what we are saved from.

Off the bat, we know that we are saved from hell. And really, all the consequences of sin for that matter. But is that it? Are we saved from anything else? Beyond that, we could claim that we are not just saved from the consequences of sin, but from sin itself, as Paul explained in the sixth chapter of Romans.

In fact, the word "saved" is the Greek word *sozo*, which has a pretty definitive meaning. *Sozo* means *"to deliver, to heal, to rescue, to make safe, and to make sound."* The word is used in a variety of ways in relation to a variety of circumstances. When Jesus encountered the mad man of Gadara, for instance, we are told that he was *saved* by Jesus when the demons were cast out of him. When Paul preached the gospel in Lystra, a crippled man in the crowd who had never walked had faith to be *saved* from his infirmity, and leaped to his feet, praising God. When Jairus' daughter died, she was *saved* from death by Jesus, and raised back to life. When a Christian says that they are saved, this means so much more than simply "destined for heaven." When you claim to be saved, understand that you are confessing before heaven and earth that your body is free from sickness, that your mind is free from torment, and that your life is His. You are saved.

And we are told that we are saved *by grace*. It is grace, that evasive Christianese concept, which holds the power of deliverance, safety, peace, healing, and salvation. Grace saves us.

And still, it does so much more.

> *"For if by the one man's offense (Adam) death reigned through the one, much more those who receive abundance of grace and of the gift of righteousness will reign in life through the One, Jesus Christ."* (Romans 5:17)

Not only does grace deliver us from humiliating defeat, but it ushers us into triumphant victory. It is through grace that we will reign. And man, am I looking forward to reigning someday in heaven. I'm not exactly sure what heaven will be like, but I know for a fact that I'm going to have an awesome job up there that involves playing Ultimate Frisbee with Jesus (that isn't a joke; I am quite looking forward to Jesus' epic diving catches). I can hardly wait until I get to reign in paradise with Jesus.

And yet, that isn't what this verse says. We are told that grace equips us to reign *in life*. Here. On earth. You see, God's grace doesn't just free us from evil. It places us in a position of authority in this present life. That God-given power that flows through your veins is in there as a result of the grace of God. Your righteous standing as a child of the Most High is a byproduct of grace. Grace is what makes you awesome! Grace is what causes you to win in every single thing you do.

By grace have you been saved, and by grace will you reign in life as an heir of Yahweh.

> *"And because you are sons, God has sent forth the Spirit of His Son into your hearts, crying out, 'Abba, Father!' Therefore you are no longer a slave but a son, and if a son, then an heir of God through Christ." (Galatians 4:7)*

Over and over and over again the Holy Spirit communicates to us through the Bible that we are *heirs* of God. In Romans chapter 8, Paul goes as far as to claim that we are "heirs of God" and "joint heirs with Christ." As a child of God, you are an heir of God, meaning you are the beneficiary of a heavenly inheritance upon someone's death. Well, who died? Jesus, the Son of Man, did. And upon His death, you received *His* inheritance. That intimate relationship Jesus shared with His Dad, the unquenchable authority Jesus walked in on a daily basis, the supernatural life of miracles Jesus lived… all of that belongs to *you* now!

When we are told that grace causes us to reign in life through

Jesus, that means we are supposed to live *like* Jesus. God's intention from the beginning was for us to be "in His likeness." Grace makes that possible. You can live *just like Him*. Ephesians 1 says that this glorious inheritance is *in us*. Furthermore, Jesus said that His impending death brought us to where He was:

> *"'And if I go to prepare a place for you, I will come again and receive you to Myself; that where I am, there you may be also.'" (John 14:3)*

And His beloved disciple John expounded upon this promise, claiming that "as He is, so are we in this world" (1 John 4:17). As He is, so are we. As He is, so are we. Jesus, up in heaven, seated at the right hand of Abba Daddy, glorified and victorious and mighty and perfect, is how *you* are. Now. In this world. I don't care what you see when you look in the mirror. God sees you the same way He sees His only begotten Son. You are just as much His kid as Jesus. You are a joint-heir, a brother (or sister) to the Son of Man.

God really did mean it when He said you were *together* with Christ, alive, raised up, and seated in the heavenly throne room of God.

Because He died, you are just like Him. Grace says so.

Paul's Thorn

We're making good progress on our quest for a better understanding of grace, but unfortunately, there is a well-known passage of scripture that will sort of throw a wrench in our discussion.

> *"And lest I should be exalted above measure by the abundance of the revelations, a thorn in the flesh was given to me, a messenger of Satan to buffet me, lest I be exalted above measure. Concerning this thing I pleaded with the Lord three times that it might depart from me. And He said to me, 'My*

grace is sufficient for you, for My strength is made perfect in weakness.' Therefore most gladly I will rather boast in my infirmities, that the power of Christ may rest upon me." (2 Corinthians 12:7-9)

Most of us are far too familiar with this tragic tale. God plagues young Paul with a terminal illness, and after Paul repeatedly begs to be healed, God turns him down, simply replying, "My grace is sufficient for you." After having this same conversation three times, Paul finally learns to live with this physical impairment, which he sees as a triumphant emblem of God's strength, and gladly bears it as a badge of honor.

Or at least that's how most of us have had the story relayed to us.

I don't really like that interpretation. Not one bit. For one, it makes grace, the source of God's salvation and power, into some sort of cheap consolation prize. Paul wanted healing; he settled for grace. Rather than giving Paul the deliverance he so desperately desired, God asked him to be content with sickness and misery instead. That doesn't sound like our loving Daddy, now, does it?

Another problem that I have with this interpretation is that, quite frankly, that version of the story just isn't true.

First of all, we must ask ourselves, or rather ask the scriptures, what Paul's "thorn in the flesh" was. A quick word-search of the scriptures shows us that thorns were used symbolically throughout the Old Testament. Thorns were used to describe the temptation to follow false gods (Numbers 33:55); they were used to describe unnecessarily laborious work (Genesis 3:18); and they were used to describe violent persecution from unbelievers (Joshua 23:13, Judges 2:3). One thing they were never used to describe: sickness. Not once. There is not a single biblical reference to thorns metaphorically representing an illness of any kind. Now Paul, a Hebrew of the Hebrews and a Pharisee in knowledge of the law, who studied under the great Gamaliel himself, would certainly be aware of the imagery his language would evoke.

Based on this new revelation, Paul's thorn would be the

persecution he suffered at the hands of unbelievers, which made his ministry journeys difficult. This seems consistent with Paul's ministry, which was wrought with multiple waves of persecution. This also seems consistent with the rest of Paul's second letter to the Corinthians. Just before he laments over his thorn in the flesh, Paul describes with great detail the persecution he had suffered over the past several years. He tells of beatings, stonings, stripes, starvation, weariness and toil, shipwrecks, and a great many other things, which he summarizes as "the things concerning *my infirmity*" (2 Corinthians 11:30).

Paul's thorn in the flesh, this mysterious infirmity, *must* have been persecution. What else depicted his ministry so vividly? What was a greater hindrance to his preaching of the gospel? What more could Paul have wanted deliverance from?

And on a logical note, how could we for one second believe that Paul had been frequently sick, given that his ministry was characterized by healing miracles? Based on a contextual reading of the scriptures, we must conclude that Paul's thorn was persecution by the Jews, and not some incurable disease.

But still, this doesn't give us a better understanding of grace. After all, who cares if the thorn is physical beatings or terminal illness? Either way, Paul begged God to deliver him, and God seemingly ignored the request, only giving Paul some meager grace to hold him over in the midst of his trials. Where is the *sozo*-salvation that grace supposedly brings?

Turning to another grace-passage will shed some light upon our dim understanding of the grace of God. And we will find this verse just a few chapters before Paul's infamous thorn.

> *"And God is able to make all grace abound toward you, that you, always having all sufficiency in all things, may have an abundance for every good work." (2 Corinthians 9:8)*

I absolutely love Paul's overuse of superlatives.

God's grace abounds toward us. Do you know what "abound" means? In the original language it was used to describe an amount that was beyond our ability to measure. Now, scientists and physicists have discovered ways to quantify the volume of the ocean, the weight of the sun, even the matter in the known universe. We can measure pretty much anything, regardless of its size. And yet, none of those exceedingly large numbers are able to aptly explain even the smallest fraction of God's grace toward you.

And this ever-abundant grace, which overflows from the throne of God, out of the heavenlies and directly into you, is said to *always* give you *all* sufficiency in *all* things.

How often is God's grace available? Always.

How sufficient is this grace? All sufficient.

And in what areas of life does this grace apply? All of them.

The vibe I get from this verse is far different than the vibe I'm told to get from the passage concerning Paul's thorn. When I hear folks talk about Paul's thorn in the flesh, the atmosphere in the room usually changes. Things start to get dim as the colors and life are sucked from the room like a high-powered vacuum. The temperature seems to drop a couple degrees, and suddenly God seems a little less *good*.

> "Yes, I know you're going to lose your house. Yup, and I'm so sorry your wife's health is getting worse. But just remember Paul's thorn in the flesh. God's grace is sufficient for you. I know that won't pay the medical bills, but maybe it'll give you some inner peace. I'll be sending my thoughts toward you."

And yet, when I read about God's abundant grace which abounds towards me, I want to climb to the roof of my office building and start screaming praises to the God who does all things well, my Savior who never leaves nor forsakes, the King of kings and Lord of lords who does the impossible just for fun.

Which God is He? The God of More-Than-Enough, or the God of Hope-That's-Enough?

In comparing the two passages, you'll see that two words appear in each verse. We see the topic of both verses is "grace."

But notice that grace is described as being "sufficient" in both passages. Look up the definition of "sufficient" in a concordance, and you'll be pleasantly surprised.

> *"A perfect condition of life in which no aid or support is needed."*

When God told Paul that grace was sufficient, He wasn't saying, "Sorry, pal, but you'll have to learn to adapt to a life of pain." On the contrary! God was saying to Paul, "Listen, I've already given you the abundance of grace. That's all you need to be delivered. I've given you every single thing you could possibly need. My grace is sufficient."

God's grace gives you absolutely everything you'll ever need. Once you receive grace there is nothing else you'll ever need. That's why Jesus said, "It is finished," as He died upon the cross of Calvary. No more work is required of God. No more sacrifice is needed. The price has been paid for grace, and this is the gateway to everything you could ever ask for or require.

When God said, "My grace is sufficient," He wasn't telling Paul, "No, I won't help you." He was saying, "Yes, I *already* have helped you." Grace wasn't the consolation prize; grace was the solution. Grace was the answer to Paul's prayer. Grace was his key to sozo-salvation.

Grace means you already have everything you will ever need from God.

The Unfair Advantage

So then, how shall we define grace?

If you look it up in a dictionary, you'll find something like this:

> *"The divine assistance and power given to man in spiritual rebirth and sanctification."*

Look it up in a concordance, and you'll get this:

> *"The merciful kindness by which God, exerting His holy influence upon souls, turns them to Christ, keeps, strengthens, increases them in Christian faith, knowledge, affection, and kindles them to the exercise of the Christian virtues."*

That's quite a mouthful. I like it, but it'd be rather tough to convey in an effective way. I've heard this definition of grace summarized as such:

> *"The divine influence on your soul, and its reflection in your life."*

Or simply:

> *"The power to live a transformed life."*

And of course, the first definition I was ever given,

> *"God's riches at Christ's expense."*

This basically means, "*We get everything Jesus has because He died for us.*" It's every blessing associated with the completed work of Christ.

So, how would I define it? How would I define the grace of God, the all-powerful force by which we are delivered from darkness and called to reign in every moment of every day?

Grace is everything you will ever need to live the awesome life that God has destined you to live.

Picture Batman storming across the rooftops of the colossal skyscrapers that line Gotham City. No matter what villainous mastermind attacks him, no matter what unexpected plague befalls him, he cannot be defeated so long as he has his trusted utility belt strapped around his waist. Grace is Batman's utility belt. It's Hal Jordan's Green Lantern ring. It's Kal-El's yellow sun, Thor's hammer, Captain America's shield, Tony Stark's suit.

Grace is your unfair advantage in life.

Understand that, above all else. Grace means you cannot lose. You are destined for victory. It's like the game is rigged, but in a totally legal way. You have God on your side. Rather, you are on His side. And His heavenly host is undefeated. Enjoy the spoils of war.

If you haven't yet seen *The Avengers*, stop reading this, go buy it, absorb the awesomeness that is that movie, and then finish this chapter.

Toward the end of the film when all hope seems lost, Tony Stark, in a visually stunning display of selfless sacrifice, commandeers a nuclear missile and flies it through an interdimensional portal to destroy the invading army of extraterrestrial crusaders (like I said, *awesome*). Stark's Iron Man suit loses power as he loses consciousness, and as he slowly plummets toward the closing portal, the audience is left to wonder if he will make it back to our galaxy before the portal closes, and if so, what will stop his terminal velocity plunge from the deep recesses of space. Will Iron Man survive?

It was quite dramatic, except for one fact. The sequel, *Iron Man 3*, had already been announced months before. As you can't have an Iron Man movie without Iron Man, everyone in that midnight premiere already knew that Iron Man would survive his daring rescue. Sure, Iron Man took a few hits, but all in all, we knew he'd be okay.

Likewise, our ultimate fate has also been announced. *Kyle is more than a conqueror. God gives Rachel the victory. Lindsey does greater works than these. Nothing will by any means hurt Cameron. All things are possible for _____.* Fill in your name. We know how it ends. Flip to the last page of the book. You win! Sure, you might take a few punches now and then, but the life you're currently living is already recorded in the history books of heaven. And spoiler alert! God says you can't lose!

Your destiny is to succeed. Your calling is to prevail. Christ our King marches before you, and a legion of angels stand behind. Whatever the battle, whatever the situation, you cannot lose. You are unquestionably supposed to win in every single area of your life. This fight isn't yours, but the Lord's. And the battle is already won.

Grace is your unfair advantage.

Final Thoughts

Months after writing this, I am still finding areas of my life where I feel undeserving of what God has given me. It's a subtle lie that was planted in my mind decades ago. Whenever you feel unworthy, like you're not good enough, like you have something to prove, stop what you're doing and pray this prayer to your Dad.

Dad, thank You for everything You have given to me. I know that I am worthy of everything you have done for me. Not because of anything I have done, but because of the blood of Christ which has cleansed me from all sin. Because of Jesus, I have access to everything that belongs to You. I am worthy because of the blood of Jesus. I thank You that my mind is continually renewed to Your truth, and that every day, I understand more and more exactly how valuable I am in Your eyes. You are so good, God. Thank You for making me good too. Amen.

Small Group Questions

1. How does this chapter relate to what you're currently reading in the bible?

2. To the best of your ability, define grace.

3. What are three things grace has saved us from?

4. What are three things grace has given us?

5. How do we know Paul's "thorn in the flesh" wasn't sickness?

6. In what ways does grace give you an unfair advantage in life?

7. Read 2 Corinthians 9:8. What is one notable thing about this verse?

8. What was the main point of this chapter?

10

My Least Favorite Bible Story

As I begin writing this chapter, I'm in the midst of studying for Friday night's sermon. For as long as I can remember we've held our youth group service on Fridays, with Cheyne and I taking turns preaching every other week. Well, this week is my turn, and I am quite excited to share. For several years we've been teaching along the lines of monthly themes (January is "Evangelism," February is "Purity," etc.), which has proven to be a huge hit with the teens. And this month the theme is "Favorite Bible Stories."

My heart leaps at the endless possibilities. I could share about Jehu, the ancient predecessor to Vin Diesel's character in "The Fast and the Furious" film series, whose epic tale is chronicled in Second Kings, chapters nine and ten.

Then there's Benaiah, of course, whose many valiant deeds are recorded for all eternity in a mere paragraph in First Chronicles.

> *"He killed two lion-like heroes of Moab."* (1 Chronicles 11:22)

It gets even better.

> *"He also killed a lion. In a pit. On a snowy day."* (1 Chronicles 11:22)

And I've always been a huge fan of Ehud, the fearless judge of Israel, who covertly travels across enemy lines, talks his way past the guards on duty (think James Bond in a tunic), and gains access into the secret chambers of the treacherous and obese King Eglon, only to impale the king with a hidden sword while he's on the toilet and steal away into the night, whilst the security team is busy arguing over the smell that is emitted from the restroom. (Judges 3)

Jephthah's a stud, Jael is diabolical (in the best of ways), and I love, love, *love* Elisha. In fact, if I were to name all of the awesome heroes of faith whose stories are told throughout the scriptures, we'd have another translation of the bible on our hands (my translation would overuse the words "awesome," "epic," and "legit"). All that to say, I had quite a few choices in front of me.

So imagine my surprise when God told me that my sermon was to be entitled, "My Least Favorite Bible Story." Not realizing I had a *least* favorite bible story, God directed me to the well-known passage colloquially known as "the parable of the Good Samaritan."

If you'll recall the story, Jesus has just finished explaining the two most important commandments, *Love God with all that you have to offer*, and *Love your neighbor*, when a man in the crowd seeks clarification on *who*, exactly, his neighbor is. Jesus responds with this story.

> *"A certain man went down from Jerusalem to Jericho, and fell among thieves, who stripped him of his clothing, wounded him, and departed, leaving him half dead. Now by chance a certain priest came down that road. And when he saw him, he passed by on the other side.*
>
> *"Likewise a Levite, when he arrived at the place, came and looked, and passed by on the other side.*
>
> *"But a certain Samaritan, as he journeyed, came where he was. And when he saw him, he had compassion. So he went to him and bandaged his wounds, pouring on oil and wine; and he set him on his own animal, brought him to an inn, and took care of him.*

> *"On the next day, when he departed, he took out two denarii, gave them to the innkeeper, and said to him, 'Take care of him; and whatever more you spend, when I come again, I will repay you.'"* (Luke 10:30-35)

Wow. That is a tall order. The generosity we find in the Good Samaritan is unparalleled. Thank goodness Jesus doesn't actually expect us to live up to that description of love. After all, this is just a parable, right? An extreme hyperbole meant to prove a point, but that is obviously far beyond what any rational Deity would expect of His subjects.

> *"[Jesus then asked] 'So which of these three do you think was neighbor to him who fell among the thieves?'" And the lawyer said, 'He who showed mercy on him.' Then Jesus said to him,* **'Go and do likewise.'**" (Luke 10:36-37)

The W-Word

Funny thing about Jesus. He actually expects us to *do stuff*.

This comes as quite a shock to most of us. After all, in today's day and age, everything is about *you*, isn't it? That's why it's called an *iPod*. That's why the customer is always right. That's why facebook was created. All to glorify *you*.

And God Himself said that we could never do anything to earn this great salvation which we have received.

> *"For by grace you have been saved through faith, and that not of yourselves; it is the gift of God, not of works, lest anyone should boast."* (Ephesians 2:8-9)

And somehow, through this odd combination of God's free gift of grace and the world's glorification of self, we have come to the conclusion that absolutely nothing is ever to be expected of us. But did you know that God actually expects us to… do… good… works?

Hopefully you've regained consciousness by now. Allow me to apologize. Here you are, reading a *Christian* book, when all of a sudden without warning, the author decides to throw out the "W-word." I know, I know, the *Christianese Dictionary* expressly forbids the use of *that* word. I mean, simply saying that word (*"works"*) implies that the grace of God wasn't enough, and that we must somehow have to *do something* to earn our own salvation.

At least that's what we've been told. But notice what the Apostle Paul said next.

> *"For by grace you have been saved through faith, and that not of yourselves; it is the gift of God, not of works, lest anyone should boast. For we are His workmanship,* **created in Christ Jesus for good works**, *which God prepared beforehand that we should walk in them." (Ephesians 2:8-10)*

You see, we aren't saved *by* good works, but according to the scriptures we are saved *for* good works. This makes perfect sense. Think about it. Why are you *still* here? As soon as you were adopted into God's family, why didn't He just whisk you off to heaven? Why leave you here on this boring, dangerous, sin-wrought planet?

The reason is obvious. *You have a job to do.* Before time was created, God mapped out the things that He wanted you to accomplish during your brief stay on planet earth. And now you are here. And there's work to be done. And as Paul so bluntly put it, "you should walk in them." That indicates that it is *your* responsibility to get cracking. The ball is in your court.

I love the language that Paul uses to describe this life of good works which God has so meticulously laid out before us. The first thing he does is inform us that our heavenly Dad is also a purveyor of good works. He created you, after all. And you are His greatest work. And just as your Dad is a worker, so you, His precious child, are called to pick up the family trade.

The word "workmanship" is a tremendously beautiful word. It is the Greek word *poiema*, where we get the word (you guessed it) "poem." But it's so much more than a simple haiku. It is used to describe a brilliant symphony, a grand masterpiece, a world-renowned artist's *magnum opus*. Think Beethoven's Fifth, Fitzgerald's *The Great Gatsby*, Christopher Nolan's *The Dark Knight Rises*. You were painstakingly designed in the mind of God eons ago for the greater works which God has prepared for you to do.

Whenever I read this verse, I picture a large orchestra gathered together in some extravagant venue like the Sydney Opera House in Australia. Dozens of musicians with a variety of instruments I can't even begin to name are littered across the stage. Violins, clarinets, trumpets, a grand piano, maybe even an oboe or two. God is the conductor, and when the band is ready He steps up to the podium, taps His baton, and signals the beginning of the performance.

If every musician follows the music written before their eyes and the precise guidance of the conductor, the sound that follows is truly divine. But all it takes is one soloist missing a note or the tuba player going off script, and the entire concert is ruined. And the bible very clearly tells us that there are pages of sheet music set before us which God intends for us to play. As members of His church, we are also members of His orchestra, and if we miss our cue or fail to play our part, what effect will that have on the presentation of the gospel to the world?

Free to Serve

So what is it that we are supposed to be doing, exactly? This mighty work that God has scrupulously set before His church, this grand symphony which He has invited us to partake in, these so-called "good works" that you and I are called to do?

It's simple, really. In a single word:

Multiply.

This primal call goes all the way back to the very beginning of time and space. The first thing we hear God say to his newborn child in Eden is this simple command. *Multiply.* This command could, of course, be interpreted to refer solely to sexual reproduction, and for a long time that was exactly how the ancient Israelites read it. They had received so great a salvation and had been welcomed into Yahweh's family, and... that was the end of it. No need to spread those seeds of faith around. No need to kindle the fire and watch it spread. No need to invite the lost and weary out from the rain. Israel was a greedy toddler on the playground, showing off his brand-new tricycle but staunchly refusing to let any of the other kids have a ride. Israel had the light, but kept it hidden safely and wastefully under a bushel. The rest of the world was in complete chaos, but they and theirs had *sozo*-salvation and that was enough for them.

I think it's easy for Christians to fall into this same pit trap. After all, we've just spent the last nine chapters of this book talking about how great *you* are. *You* are deeply loved by God. *You* have God living on the inside. *You* have been made new, been made clean, been made perfect, been made good. The blood of Christ has made *you* worthy. *You* have everything you need. *You* are just like God. Let's face it, *you* are pretty hot stuff. And when we get to talking about how awesome and spectacular and amazing *you* are, it's easy to lose sight of everybody else.

But *everybody else* is exactly why you are still here. And I'd argue that *everybody else* is part of the reason God has made your life so stinking awesome. Flip back to the original promise God made to Abraham, the future father of His kingdom:

> "'I will make you a great nation; I will bless you and make your name great; and you shall be a blessing.'" (Genesis 12:2)

Sure, God promised to abundantly bless the crud out of Abraham, and yes, He also pledged to make his name great, but then He attached a stipulation to it. *You shall be a blessing.* Wait, God, you mean that the blessing you gave us was intended to bless *others* as well?

There's a lot of talk in the body of Christ today concerning prosperity. Some Christians think it's wrong to be rich, and others think it's wrong to be poor. The plain and simple truth is that God wants his people abundantly provided for. Remember, we're Batman and God is Dr. Wayne. And any honest reading of the scriptures clearly demonstrates that God has no problem with money; He only takes issue with greed. Living paycheck to paycheck is not God's plan. But God's plan is also not for you to have six flat-screens in your garage while your neighbor struggles to pay the mortgage. You are supposed to be a blessing to those around you.

Margaret Thatcher so astutely pointed out, "No one would remember the Good Samaritan if he'd only had good intentions; he had money as well." Paul says this same thing to his protégé, Timothy:

> *"Command those who are rich in this present age not to be haughty, nor trust in uncertain riches but in the living God, who gives us richly all things to enjoy. Let them do good, that they be rich in good works, ready to give, willing to share." (1 Timothy 6:17-18)*

Notice that we are first told to *enjoy* the things God has freely given us. We're not simply God's money launderer, throwing His favor out to the masses and living off the scraps. God wants your life to be fantastic. He wants you taken care of. Abundantly provided for. But He wants so much more than that. He has changed *your* world; now He wants you to go change the world around you.

Think back to the words that Jesus spoke in the eleventh chapter of Matthew. He called those who were tired and heavy laden to come to Him and promised that He would carry their burdens and give them rest. Peter reminds us of this promise years later, inviting us to "cast our cares on Him, because He cares for us" (1 Peter 5:7). Why do you think Jesus took our burdens? On the one hand it was because those weights were *heavy*. Jesus wanted to liberate us from the oppression that had been laid on us all those years ago. But it wasn't just so we could walk around, burden-free and livin' the life.

> *"Bear one another's burdens, and so fulfill the law of Christ."* (Galatians 6:2)

Maybe Jesus didn't take all your cares and anxieties and worries just for your own comfort. Maybe it was so your hands would be free to help *others* in need. Maybe, just maybe, it was so you could show the love of Christ to a dark and dying world. Maybe it wasn't *just* for you.

I don't know if it's funny or sad how much the Israelites missed it. I mean, it was right in front of them. Israel wasn't meant to be this exclusive country club of a nation, hoarding God all to themselves. They were supposed to be a beacon of hope to the world, the means by which the rest of the nations could know the Creator of the universe. Instead, they were puffed up with spiritual pride and became so self-centric that when God showed up in the flesh, they refused to recognize Him. They then demanded that their Savior be crucified, all so they could maintain their selfish, religious practices without interference. But their relationship with God was never intended to be solely for them. In fact, God said that saving *only* Israel wasn't nearly an impressive enough feat for Almighty God.

> *"It is too small a thing that you should be my servant to raise up the tribes of Jacob, and to restore the preserved ones of Israel; I will also give you as a light to the Gentiles, that you should be My salvation to the ends of the earth."* (Isaiah 49:6)

God's children are the lightning bugs of truth. We're the searchlights of hope. We're the torchbearers of love. So why do we try so hard cover that light up? Why do we try to keep it all to ourselves? Let us come out of hiding, strip off those burdensome bushels, and allow this light to shine out into the darkness, that the world would see our good works, and glorify our Dad.

Full

My office is about twenty miles from our home. As such, I take a trip over to the gas station about once a week. I drive a pickup truck, which means filling that tank could potentially be an upsetting process, if not for the confidence I have in God's overly abundant provision. The "Price" tally always seems to outrun the "Gallons" tally, and by a larger margin every time, but like I said, God is good, so I don't stress it. Not one bit.

But let's suspend reality, and pretend for a moment that I worked from home. Would I still be visiting the Chevron off of Trabuco and El Toro every Thursday morning? Of course not! The only reason I fill up my tank every week is because I intend to use the gas that is provided.

Or if I'm at a restaurant with my family, I only expect the waiter to fill my water cup after I've drank from it. If my cup is already full, there'd be no reason for the waiter to fill it. In fact, if I don't intend on drinking from the cup, one might question why I had it filled in the first place.

So here's the question I'm posing to you: *Why do you think you've been filled?*

We read throughout the bible that we've been filled with the Holy Spirit (Ephesians 5:18). We've been filled with joy (John 16:24). We've been filled with glory (1 Peter 1:8) and riches (1 Corinthians 4:8) and goodness and knowledge (Romans 15:14) and love (Romans 5:5). We've even been filled with all the fullness of God (Ephesians 3:19). And that's just the tip of the iceberg.

So my question is *why*? Why fill you up? Why top off the tank? If this vessel of God is just going to sit in the driveway for all eternity, what's the point? It seems that the only reason you'd fill something up is if it's supposed to do something. I only fill up my truck when I need to *go* to some place, or to someone. Funny, that was Jesus' final command. *Go.*

Jesus described the concept of being *full* of the Holy Spirit in two different ways. The first was when He struck up a conversation with the Samaritan woman at the Well of Jacob. After playfully discussing the nutritional benefits of dihydrogen monoxide, Jesus throws this metaphysical offer out there:

> *"'Whoever drinks of the water that I shall give him will never thirst. But the water that I shall give him will become in him a fountain of water springing up into everlasting life.'" (John 4:14)*

Of course, the "water" that Jesus is referring to is the Holy Spirit. In this passage, Jesus is describing the work of the Holy Spirit for salvation. And the Holy Spirit is depicted as a fountain within the believer, providing the fresh waters of eternal life for the believer. And this fresh water, this salvation, is contained within the believer.

Yet just a couple weeks later, Jesus describes the Holy Spirit in a slightly different way.

> *"'If anyone thirsts, let him come to Me and drink. He who believes in Me, as the Scripture has said, out of his heart will flow rivers of living water.'" (John 7:37-38)*

It's practically the same metaphor. The Holy Spirit is again typified as water. But this time, it's not a fountain. It's a river. Correction: *rivers*. Plural. And this isn't some peaceful stream, softly flowing in the breeze behind your grandmother's house. This is an overwhelming torrent, a violent, tumultuous wall of waves. Elsewhere, Jesus used this same word to describe the dangerous floods that vehemently beat down the ill-prepared homes lining the Jordan River. And that is the power of the Holy Spirit within you.

But unlike the gentle fountain springing up inside of you for your own personal salvation, these rivers were never meant to be contained. Jesus said that this work of the Holy Spirit was designed to flow *out* of your very being. Right now, as you are reading the words on this page, the waves of love and freedom are crashing back and forth throughout your spirit, desperately waiting for the floodgates to be opened so that the Holy Spirit can pour out of your hands and feet and lips, and flood the barren wasteland that is your community.

The Holy Spirit is inside. And He's just waiting to be let out.

This Little Light o' Mine

Jesus made a pretty cool statement in the eighth chapter of John.

> *"'I am the light of the world. He who follows Me shall not walk in darkness, but have the light of life.'" (John 8:12)*

Who is the Light? Jesus. Obviously.

Who else? Are there any other lights around these here parts? If not, we're going to have some trouble, because Jesus is seated up in heaven right now. But luckily, before confusion sets in we can turn to the red-lettered words of Jesus to shed some light on the discussion at hand.

> *"'You are the light of the world.'" (Matthew 5:14)*

I guess that sort of settles it, huh? You and I are lights in this world. It makes sense when you think it through. After all, Pastor James called God the "Father of Lights" (James 1:17). That means there is more than one light to which He is the Progenitor. We also know that at the moment of our salvation, we became just like God. And since He is *The* Light, we too are lights here on earth.

So, great. We are lights. Whoop-de-doo. What does that mean, exactly? Again, we've stumbled upon one of those truths that has become diluted through centuries of neglect. What is this so-called "light" that we are supposed to be?

We find that answer by going back to the beginning. John's rendition of the beginning, to be specific.

"In the beginning was the Word, and the Word was with God, and the Word was God... in Him was life, and the life was the light of men." (John 1:1, 4)

The light of men is the life of God.

That comes as quite a relief because as we discussed extensively several chapters ago, we already *have* that life. That *zoe*-life, that God-kind-of-Life, that everlasting life that flows through our veins, pumps through our heart, and keeps us alive is the source of our salvation. And we are instructed to allow that life of God, that *light*, to penetrate and permeate the sheer darkness of this lost and dying world.

How exactly do you do this? Well, I can tell you how you *don't* do it. You don't let your light shine by gossiping about the people you know. You don't shine that light by complaining about your bosses, teachers, or parents. You certainly don't do it by living just like the lost. We are called to a higher standard of living, and maintaining that righteous standard is only made possible by the life of God within us.

But it's more than just behaving morally and following all of the rules. It's residing in a higher plane of existence. It's transcending the cares of this fading world. It's living with God. When you live your day-to-day life constantly in the presence of your loving Dad, it transforms everything about you. It changes the way you speak. It changes the way you act. It changes the way you think. Heck, it even changes the way you look.

Over three thousand years ago, Moses stood atop Mount Sinai in the very presence of Yahweh. When Moses came down from that literal mountaintop experience, we read that his face radiated the glory of God. People couldn't even look at him because he was shining so brightly. Jesus, too, hiked up a mountain with His disciples to spend time with God, and His appearance shifted into something the disciples could neither describe nor gaze upon. I've read stories that Smith Wigglesworth would walk into buildings and the atmosphere inside would change. Men would see Wigglesworth coming and without a word fall to their knees and

My Least Favorite Bible Story

repent, for a man of God had entered the building.

I don't know if I've ever physically glowed before, but I do remember a similar experience that has stuck with me for years.

It was my senior year in high school, and I had been a Christian for less than half a year. During those first six months, I had changed drastically, though I had hardly noticed. One afternoon I was hanging out with an old friend of mine. This guy was one of the most popular kids in school. He was the star of the football and basketball teams, and had been voted athlete of the year. He was with a different girl every week and was center stage at a different party every weekend. From a worldly standpoint, this guy had everything going for him.

I was literally the opposite. When I got saved I lost most of my friends. I stopped playing high school basketball and club soccer and spent my weekends at church. Don't get me wrong, I was completely satisfied with my new life with God, but I figured my life wasn't very appealing to those outside the church.

Anyway, I was hanging out with this guy, assuming that he thought I was the dorkiest guy on the planet, when his countenance suddenly changed. He looked at me, and with tears in his eyes he said to me, "What is it that you have?"

At first, I didn't know what the heck he was talking about.

"What is it that you have that I don't have? I don't know what it is, but there is something about your life that I don't have. And I need it. Badly."

What I had was an intimate friendship with the God of the universe. And though this kid had no interest in God and had filled his life with girls and drugs and alcohol and partying, he could still see that bright light shining through the darkness.

That story isn't intended to glorify me. I did nothing. In fact, I was oblivious to the fact that Christ was shining through me. But when you live life with your loving Savior, it's impossible that the world *won't* see Him.

Paul explained it so simply to Philemon.

> "[I pray] that the sharing of your faith may become effective

> *by the acknowledgement of every good thing which is in you in Christ Jesus."* (Philemon 6)

Paul gives us such an insight into effective evangelism in this single verse. When others notice the good things God has placed *within* you, your effectiveness in evangelism shoots through the roof. It's not just the things that you *do*. Usually it has more to do with who you are.

That's not to say that *doing stuff* is not important. Au contraire, it's incredibly important, and the focus of the remainder of this book. But the things we do should be done in light of the life God has given us. James tells us this rather bluntly.

> *"Who is wise and understanding among you? Let him show by good conduct that his works are done in the meekness of wisdom."* (James 3:13)

A more literal (and accurate) translation of this verse would read something like:

> "Let him show by *a life lived in the midst of the people* that his works come directly from *His heavenly Father.*"

The life of God is the light of men. And that light is supposed to be lighting up every single thing we do, for the entire world to see.

Light and Works

We have a lot of Christians who are doing tons of work, but they are working without the life of God shining through it. We also have a lot of Christians who are well aware of the life of God within, but they aren't actually doing anything (much like our Hebrew predecessors). And I don't mean to show disrespect to either camp, but Jesus tells us that neither one is right.

My Least Favorite Bible Story

> *"'Let your light so shine before men, that they may see your good works and glorify your Father in heaven.'" (Matthew 5:16)*

Having light is not enough. Plenty of Christians have light. And their churches are very well lit. But they keep that power locked up in the four walls of their church building and wonder why the rest of the city is shrouded in darkness.

Doing works isn't enough. There are plenty of Christians doing good deeds. And yes, the work that some are doing is fabulous work, and I have the utmost respect for all those working to make the world a better place. But if God is only there in name, but not there in power and presence, the work that you are doing is no different than the work that charitable atheists are doing.

But follow the equation that Jesus gave us and watch what happens. It's a pretty easy formula.

$$\frac{\begin{array}{c}\text{Light}\\+\\\text{Works}\end{array}}{\text{Revival}}$$

And that, my friend, is how you change the world.

Final Thoughts

It's so easy to get bogged down with the cares and worries of our own lives. Make a decision today to stop worrying about your life. Trust that your Dad will actually care for you like a father cares for his kids, and say this prayer.

God, I trust You with my entire life. My family, my friends, my school, my job, my finances. Everything. Today I make a decision NOT to worry about these things. Whatever I need, I know that You will provide it for me. And since I am not worrying about my own life, show me how I can be a blessing in someone else's life today. Lead me to someone who is in desperate need of Your love today. Give me wisdom that I would know how to handle the situation. Holy Spirit, speak through me today as I bless the people around me today. Use me today, God.

Now go bless someone. Make a difference in their world.

Small Group Questions

1. How does this chapter relate to what you're currently reading in the bible?

2. When Jesus said, "Go and do likewise," what was He telling us to do?

3. Why do some people think works are bad? Why do some people think works are good? What do you think?

4. Is enjoying money and material things sinful? Why or why not?

5. Why did Jesus describe the Holy Spirit differently in John 4 and John 7?

6. What is the work of the church? How can you help achieve this work?

7. Read Ephesians 2:8-10. What is one notable thing about this verse?

8. What was the main point of this chapter?

11
Change the World

Wow, we've covered quite a bit of ground, haven't we? When I started writing this book, I wasn't really sure where we'd end up. As far as I knew, I was just going on a walk with my Dad with a pen and a pad of paper, without knowing exactly where He intended to take me. Well, here we are, almost at the end of our journey. Let us take just a moment to gaze back upon the path we've been traveling upon, so that we might remember what magnificent truths we've seen thus far.

> *You were created for the singular purpose of being absolutely and unequivocally loved by God.*
>
> *God isn't your distant and angry father; He's your loving Dad, and you are His beloved child.*
>
> *You are no longer a sinner. You've been made brand new.*
>
> *As a child of the Most High, you are just like God.*
>
> *The Holy Spirit really does live inside of you (in fact, He's in there right now).*
>
> *Nothing is impossible. Literally, there is no thing you cannot do.*
>
> *Not only that, but Jesus said you can do greater works than He did (and you will)!*
>
> *Jesus' blood has made you worthy of every blessing He has*

> *given you.*
>
> *Not only has God's abundant grace saved you from sin, but it also has placed you in a position to win in every area of life.*
>
> *You have everything you will ever need to live the awesome life that God has destined you to live.*
>
> *You are destined to change the world.*

Well, that was quite a mouthful. And it's all fine and dandy. But there's a problem. Where do we go from here?

So often when I read books like this book you're holding in your hands, I become overwhelmed with excitement. *Wow, God really is great! There is nothing we can't do!* But when I reach the last page of the book, I feel sort of like a kid whose mom forgot to pick him up from soccer practice. I'm just standing alone in the parking lot. I'm not really sure what I'm supposed to do next. I'm just waiting for something to happen, for someone to show up and lead me to the next step.

Now that we know all of these fantastic truths… what are we supposed to do? And how do we get started?

While there are plenty of things I think you should do (follow me on Twitter, donate money to MountainChild, give this book to someone who needs it), I think it would be more appropriate to start with the words of Jesus.

What does Jesus want you to do?

> *"And He said to them, 'Go into all the world and preach the gospel to every creature… and these signs will follow those who believe: in My name they will cast out demons; they will speak with new tongues; they will take up serpents; and if they drink anything deadly, it will by no means harm them; they will lay hands on the sick, and they will recover.'" (Mark 16:15, 17, 18)*

Jesus tells us in no uncertain terms that we are to preach the gospel everywhere we go to everyone we meet. And not wanting us to enter the battlefield unarmed, He gives us quite the arsenal of authority.

These are but a few of the weapons loaded on that utility belt of grace we've been fitted with.

Casting Out Demons

Lots of people have lots of things to say about demons, and a multitude of books have been written on the subject, detailing the various names, powers, and origin stories of the demonic. But Jesus was fairly brief on the topic. There was really only one thing He ever said about demons:

You are so much more powerful than they are.

That's pretty much all you need to know on the topic. You have all power over them. And they don't have any power over you. Not an ounce.

I don't have any personal experience with exorcisms, but my wife has had to cast out demons several times in her life. The first time occurred when she was sixteen years old, but God, being the awesome God that He is, warned Cheyne about the experience the night before in a dream. She had dreamed that she was attacked by a demon, and in the dream she was terrified. Suddenly, she heard a calm voice speak to her during the assault: "If you tell them to go, they *have* to listen." She stood up in her dream, still gripped with fear, and boldly declared, "You must leave in the name of Jesus!" Instantly, the onslaught stopped. Then she woke up.

The next evening, Cheyne encountered her first demon-possessed girl. If you're expecting a dramatic story congruent to *The Exorcist*, complete with levitating babies and green pea soup, then you're going to be very disappointed. There was no battle. There was no climax. There was no struggle. Just a poor, helpless girl possessed of the devil. She (or rather the demon inside) taunted my wife, and tried to attack her. Cheyne stood her ground, and commanded the evil to leave. And just like that, it was over. To say God prevailed would be an understatement, for it implies the possibility of failure. It was an unfair fight from the beginning. God was with Cheyne. Who could possibly stand against that divine duo?

You have absolute authority over the devil. That's what Jesus said. But remember, this God-given power is bestowed upon us in the context of the preaching of the gospel. Jesus strictly warned His followers of the consequences of casting out demons without teaching the Word afterwards (Matthew 12:43-45). The purpose of these signs is to bring people back to their heavenly Dad, not to create a spectacle.

Now, a quick word to the wise. Not *everyone* who dislikes you is possessed by the devil. Your geometry teacher, who for whatever reason just doesn't seem to care for you very much, probably isn't demon-possessed. He's just mean. And lost. He most likely doesn't need an exorcism; he just needs an introduction to Christ. You shouldn't go searching for the devil underneath every rock, because those who do usually find him and are ill-prepared to handle it. Just know that as long as you are regularly hanging with your Dad, you will know what to do should a situation arise. Trust the Holy Spirit within you, and learn to follow His voice. He will always show you what's to come (just as He did for Cheyne), and teach you how to handle it.

Speaking in Tongues

After three years of itinerant ministry, chock full of healings and miracles and resurrections galore, after His unjust arrest, kangaroo court trial, and subsequent beating, after dying on the cross, triumphing over death itself, and appearing to His disciples and filling their heads with dreams of grandeur and the spectacular and the impossible, Jesus sat them down, and as He was about to ascend into the heavens, He gave them one final command.

Wait.

Huh?

Wait.

For what, Jesus? What could possibly be so important that You expect us to sit here and wait?

> *Wait for the Promise of the Father, the baptism of the Holy Spirit.* (Acts 1:4)

You see, all of the mighty and awesome things that God said we could do are contingent on being filled with the Holy Spirit, as we discussed in Chapter 6. Jesus knew the church could never accomplish the impossible task laid before it without the indwelling power of the Holy Spirit, so He commanded them to wait until that fateful day of Pentecost, when the Spirit of God rushed through their midst like a mighty wind, clothing them with power from on high and overflowing them with God Himself.

And the moment they were filled with the Holy Spirit, something tremendous happened.

> *"And they were all filled with the Holy Spirit and began to speak in other tongues, as the Spirit gave them utterance."* (Acts 2:4)

Every last one of them began to speak in a language beyond their own understanding. They didn't know what they were saying. They were simply obeying the parting words of Christ, and the results were astounding: three thousand lost souls joined God's family. And lest we think for a moment that this divine experience was reserved for a select few, we see over and over again that this happens to all who are filled with the Spirit.

> *"While Peter was still speaking these words, the Holy Spirit fell upon all those who heard the word. And those of the circumcision who believed were astonished, as many as came with Peter, because the gift of the Holy Spirit had been poured out on the Gentiles also. For they heard them speak with tongues and magnify God."* (Acts 10:44-46)

> *"And when Paul had laid hands on them, the Holy Spirit came upon them, and they spoke with tongues and prophesied."* (Acts 19:6)

And in the sixteenth chapter of Mark, Jesus imparts this gift to all believers. More than that, He tells us that without the baptism of the Holy Spirit and the adjoining tongue-praying, you will not be able to accomplish nearly as much as you are intended to.

Speaking in tongues brings many blessings to the life of a believer, which is why the bible repeatedly tells us to pray in the Spirit always. To name just a few of the many blessings, speaking in tongues (also called "praying in tongues" and "praying in the Spirit"):

- is speaking directly to God (1 Corinthians 14:2)
- edifies (or builds up and strengthens) yourself (1 Corinthians 14:4)
- is your spirit praying, not your mind (1 Corinthians 14:14)
- is how you can pray when you're not sure what to pray (Romans 8:26)
- builds up your faith (Jude 20)
- keeps you in the love of God (Jude 21)

Speaking in tongues was something that Paul was constantly doing, and as such, I've followed suit. I pray in tongues when I drive to work. I sing in tongues in the shower. I pray in the Spirit quietly as I walk to the copier. Heck, I'm praying in tongues right now!

I was filled with the Holy Spirit and spoke with tongues for the first time when I was a freshman in college. A couple of days later I was walking the campus of UCI after an especially troubling lecture. I was in quite a bad mood, and as I walked to my next class I decided to take God at His Word and try this whole "tongues" thing out. I figured that if speaking in tongues would really "edify" me, now was the perfect time. So in a bout of faith, I began to pray in tongues as I walked across Aldrich Park.

Two hundred seconds and four hundred paces later, I was straight-up exuberant to be alive. I was smiling – no, beaming – with delight, pumped in the Holy Spirit and ready to take the rest of my education by storm. I'm not sure exactly how to describe it, other than this: God showed up. His Word was true. And when you do the things He tells you to do, things get better. Much better.

Praying in tongues is a gift that is absolutely necessary for all believers. I can't imagine my life without it. And Jesus couldn't picture your life without it, either. That's why He suffered at Calvary to guarantee this gift would be yours.

If you're not filled with the Holy Spirit or you've never spoken in tongues before, let's take care of that today. Contact me through GarrettMilovich.com, where I can answer any questions you may have, provide you with some useful resources, and pray with you to receive the baptism of the Holy Spirit with the evidence of speaking in other tongues.

Take Up Serpents

According to Jesus, you have a bright future working as a snake charmer. Go you!

Just kidding.

This verse doesn't mean that you should go hunting for snakes when you get bored. "Serpents" refers to the works of the devil (that serpent of old), and Jesus tells us that we have complete protection from the works of the enemy. Remember back to Jesus' words to His disciples concerning the devil:

> *"'Behold, I give you the authority to trample on serpents and scorpions, and over all the power of the enemy, and nothing shall by any means hurt you.'" (Luke 10:19)*

How much authority do you have?

All.

How many things shall hurt you?

None.

Not a single thing. Not even kryptonite.

This doesn't mean that the devil won't attack. But through grace God has given you the answer to every problem the devil throws your way. And in the off-chance the devil manages to get a punch in, you already have everything you need to come out on top, be it physical healing, increased finances, forgiveness, or direction from the Holy Spirit.

Before we move on, in the final chapter of Acts Paul is actually attacked by a literal snake. After a shipwreck, Paul and his team find themselves on the island of Malta, where the natives show him and his ministry team "unusual kindness." Suddenly, Paul is attacked by a viper. The natives see this, and assume that Paul was some sort of horrible sinner suffering cosmic retribution. Hmmm. Unusual kindness? Karma? Paul is surrounded by Buddhists!

However, Paul knows something that they don't know. He has an unfair advantage in life.

> *"However, they were expecting that he would swell up or suddenly fall down dead. But after they had looked for a long time and saw no harm come to him, they changed their minds and said that he was a god." (Acts 28:6)*

I find this story fascinating. The devil tries to take out Paul in front of a heathen audience, but the unprecedented protection which only God can provide turns this dreadful occurrence into an opportunity for Paul to preach the gospel to an entire island. The natives recognize the power of God on Paul's life, and Paul in turn introduces them to his Dad.

Don't be afraid when the serpents and scorpions close in. Trust in God and believe that there really is nothing that can harm you. Then trample upon the enemy and watch as those around you flock to your King.

Deadly Drinks

Put down the mug of motor oil. This isn't a cool way to impress your friends.

Jesus promises us that we are not only immune to the spiritual attacks of the devil, but also to physical attacks as well. While Jesus only mentions *drinking* deadly things, I wouldn't limit this protection to liquids. Certainly we are also protected from eating deadly foods, and even from inhaling deadly gases. But really, as we flip through the bible we will find that we are protected from any natural assault. Jesus' statement means that we are safe from natural disasters, freak accidents, even the common cold. We have divine protection from any natural attack.

Again, Jesus said that *nothing* would *by any means* hurt you. I'd say that's all-encompassing.

This verse is very closely related to the "take up serpents" clause mentioned above. The main reason I wrote about it in a separate section is because I wanted to briefly talk about how we pray over our food. I'm sure most of us pray over our meals. And in the back of our heads we have this idea that if we forget to pray for our food, we are suddenly subject to salmonella, food poisoning, or worse. Yet Jesus very plainly said, "It will by no means harm you." If we forget to pray over our food, Jesus doesn't suddenly turn our subway sandwich into poison. Our food is already protected, whether we prayed for it or not.

So what, then? Should we stop praying over our food? Certainly not! But rather than pray out of fear of the imminent death that lies deep within the dark recesses of your kung pao chicken, we should pray out of gratitude to our loving Dad, who time and time again provides us with everything we need, be it food, finances, wisdom, or everything else on the innumerable list of daily blessings He so freely showers upon us.

Also, this promise of protection doesn't release us from common sense. If you eat McDonalds twenty-four hours a day, seven days a week, that's just stupid. Don't eat like a pig and expect God to shield you from obesity, diabetes, or heart problems. Doing that isn't faith. It's exploitation.

Lay Hands on the Sick

I don't know if you've noticed it, but I don't think I've cited *one* single verse about physical healing in this entire book. I may have subtly alluded to it several times, but I certainly didn't expound upon it. And yet, I believe I have already made a flawless case for God's unwavering desire for His people to walk in perfect health.

There are 178 distinct biblical passages about God's ability and willingness to heal (that I've found this week), but without flipping to *any* of those, I am confident in this truth: *God is a healing God*. How can you read about God's unfathomable love for His children and still believe that God is behind sickness? How can you know of God's abundant grace and still think that divine healing is not available to you? How can someone read over and over and over again the countless stories of God sweeping in and rescuing His beloved in just the nick of time, of the miracles that poured from the hands of Jesus and His disciples, of the sensational promises that abound throughout the scriptures, and yet hold on to the appalling idea that God is behind your sufferings?

There are many views that are incongruent with the bible, and the idea that sickness comes from God, or that healing isn't an option for all believers, is definitely one of them. For far too long this false doctrine has plagued the church, and countless Christians have died prematurely due to a lack of accurate information. Let God Himself be your source, for in Him and in His Word you will find the truth: God is *Jehovah Rapha, the God who heals.*

And in Jesus' final address to His followers, after telling them that they are protected from every attack of the enemy, both spiritual and physical, He gives unto them a new commission.

You will lay hands on the sick.

Who will? The pastor of your church? The televangelist? The missionary to Africa? No, Jesus said the one who believes in His name.

You.

And when you lay hands on the sick, what happens?

You will lay hands on the sick, and they will recover.

Who recovers?

They.

What a relief to know that their recovery isn't *your* responsibility. Your job isn't to figure out their ailment, diagnose it, and cure it. Your job is to simply preach the word and lay the hands. After that, your job is done.

Now I know what you're thinking. *What if it doesn't work?* But here's my question for you: why wouldn't it work? God said it, didn't He? You believe it, don't you? That should settle it. *But I don't think that it works that way.* How would you know? You've probably never prayed for the sick before, at least not with the reckless audacity of faith, so you have no reason to doubt it. If God said it and you believe it, that should settle it.

Am I saying that *everyone* who gets prayed for will be healed? Certainly not. But guess what? Not everyone Jesus prayed for was healed, either.

> "Now Jesus could do no mighty work there, except that He laid His hands on a few sick people and healed them. And He marveled because of their unbelief." (Mark 6:5, 6)

Jesus *could do* no mighty work. It doesn't say He chose not to. It says He couldn't. Do you know what that means? That means He prayed for some people, and they weren't healed. But the bible doesn't blame God's will for this failure, or even Jesus' ability. God places the responsibility solely on the people's unbelief. As I said before, your job is to do the preaching and the praying. After that, the individual does the believing and God does the healing.

And what do you suppose happened when the disciples did their job and preached the gospel to the lost?

> "And they went out and preached everywhere, the Lord working with them and confirming the word through the accompanying signs. Amen." (Mark 16:20)

Amen is right! Their obedience to Christ's commission opened the door for Him to work with them. And every word they spoke was confirmed by Christ Himself. This reiterates that your responsibility is simply to obey. You have the easy job. Leave the miracle-working to God.

These are just five of the many things that Jesus has equipped you to do during your time here on earth. Although all of these signs are spectacular, none of them are particularly unexpected. Given what we know about God and ourselves, I feel these miracles almost go without saying. Of course they are true! Why wouldn't God protect us from harm? Why wouldn't He heal and provide and deliver? After all, He is God. He can do all things. And guess what? So can you.

Go and Do Likewise

The proclamation of Jesus found in Mark 16, to go into all the world and vanquish the powers of darkness, is not a lone passage. Throughout Jesus' three year ministry, He shouted out similar orders, commanding His loyal followers to help those in need.

> *"'As you go, preach, saying, "The kingdom of heaven is at hand." Heal the sick, cleanse the lepers, raise the dead, cast out demons. Freely you have received, freely give.'"* (Matthew 10:8)

> *"'Whatever city you enter, and they receive you, eat such things as are set before you. And heal the sick there, and say to them, "The kingdom of God has come near to you."'"* (Luke 10:8-9)

> *"And Jesus came and spoke to them, saying, 'All authority has been given to Me in heaven and on earth. Go therefore and make disciples of all nations, baptizing them in the name of the Father and of the Son and of the Holy Spirit, teaching them to observe all things that I have commanded you.'"* (Matthew 28:18-20)

> *"'But you shall receive power when the Holy Spirit has come upon you; and you shall be witnesses of Me in Jerusalem, and in all Judea and Samaria, and to the end of the earth.'"* (Acts 1:8)

Notice that every single one of these statements directly connects the miraculous power of God to the preaching of His gospel. The words of God are supposed to usher forth from our mouths, and the works of God are supposed to usher forth from our hands and feet.

Of course, the works of God are not limited to the very few that I mentioned in this chapter. These are just a couple of no-brainers to get the ball rolling. But there really is no limit to what you can do. So long as you are walking with God, everything truly is possible.

One that I feel compelled to emphasize is Jesus' command to *freely give*. We, the church of the Most High God, should be known for many noble things, one of them being our extreme and outlandish generosity. Remember the unreasonably high precedent Jesus established with the story of the Good Samaritan. *Go and do likewise*. It is our duty to care for the poor, for the widows and the orphans, for the broken and the destitute. If it's any consolation, the money in your bank account isn't really yours. It all belongs to God. He's just letting you use it.

And you don't belong to yourself either, for that matter. You've been bought with a price, as the scriptures tell us, and an extremely high price at that, which demonstrates just how valuable you are to God's kingdom. Your life isn't your property, so just surrender your doubts and worries and anxieties and shortcomings, and follow after Him.

I'll end this chapter with a verse that has always caused my spirit to leap in faith within me.

> "'The law and the prophets were until John. Since that time the kingdom of God has been preached, and everyone is pressing into it. And it is easier for heaven and earth to pass away than for one tittle of the law to fail.'" (Luke 16:16-17)

Take hold of the kingdom. Rise up in faith. Step out of the boat. Dare to be fearless. Go and do likewise.

Final Thoughts

Imagine if every single morning, Christians across the world left their homes anticipating this unfathomable power of God to flow from their hands and feet. God has placed that supernatural ability inside of you. It's simply a matter of you deciding to let it out.

God, You commanded me to go into the world and preach the gospel to everyone I meet. Thank You for giving me boldness, that I would be unashamed to proclaim Your gospel. I will be strong and of good courage, for You have not given me a spirit of fear, but of power, of love, and of a sound mind. And I thank You that when I speak Your word, You confirm it with signs and wonders following. Wherever I go, I expect You to be right there with me, pouring out Your love and power. The blind will see, the deaf will hear, the lame will walk, and the sick will be healed, in the wonderful name of Jesus. Amen!

Small Group Questions

1. How does this chapter relate to what you're currently reading in the bible?

2. It what ways do you have authority over the power of the devil?

3. What are three benefits to praying in tongues?

4. What does the bible say about your supernatural protection?

5. Do Christians have the ability to heal the sick?

6. In what ways can you change the world?

7. Read Mark 16:15-20. What is one notable thing about this verse?

8. What was the main point of this chapter?

12

Kings or Priests

There are various stories recorded in the gospels that relate to us how Jesus interacted with various groups of people. We see how He acted with His disciples. We read of the parables He told them, the sermons He preached to them, the authority He bestowed upon them, and even how He defended them from the scrutiny of the religious elite. We also learn of Jesus' relationship with His family, how He submitted to and obeyed His mother and father, how He put His relationship with God first, how He made sure His family was taken care of as He took His last breaths on the cross.

But there is one story that I find most interesting, and it tells of an interaction He had with some of His friends. Lazarus, a friend of Jesus, became deathly ill, and his sisters turned to Jesus for help.

> "Now Jesus loved Martha and her sister and Lazarus. So, when He heard that Lazarus was sick, He stayed two more days in the place where He was." (John 11:5-6)

Wait, what?

Jesus' close friend is on the verge of death and so Jesus, the compassionate, miracle-working Son of God... stays right where He is. Doesn't move a muscle. Doesn't lift a finger.

If this were to happen today you had better believe that the senior pastor would be by his side in a heartbeat. That just seems like the right thing to do. It doesn't matter what you have going on, if one of your friends is lying on his death bed you drop everything and get there. But not Jesus.

Jesus, for whatever reason, chooses to tarry for *two days* before heading over. When He finally does arrive, Lazarus has already been buried. Friends and family are gathered together, grieving the premature loss of their dear friend and brother. Martha sees Jesus and is able to compose herself long enough to say, "If you had been here, my brother would not have died." And she was absolutely right. If Jesus *had* been there, Lazarus would still be alive. So what gives? Why wasn't Jesus there when any Christian in their right mind would have been?

The reason you and I and every other rational Christian would have been there is because most of us are very *evangelism-conscious*. By this, I mean that we are all very aware of the things around us. We are aware of other people's needs. We are aware of the troubles of this world. We are aware of the authority we have been granted. And as a result, we put it all together and leap into action.

But Jesus wasn't like that. He wasn't evangelism-conscious. Rather, He was *God-conscious*. He didn't move when other people demanded or when it seemed He had reached the point of no return. He moved only when God said, "Move." That doesn't mean He ignored the things around Him. But the things around Him didn't dictate His next move. His direction came from God alone.

The famous mantra we learned from a decade of Spider-Man flicks is *"With great power comes great responsibility."* You and I have been given a tremendous amount of power, and it's important for us to remember that our responsibility is to first and foremost love and follow after our Savior King.

To Be a Priest

> *"To Him who loved us and washed us from our sins in His own blood, and has made us kings and priests to His God and Father, to Him be glory and dominion forever and ever. Amen."* (Revelation 1:5-6)

What a fabulous declaration that the Apostle John speaks over

Kings or Priests

us in this chapter. He tells us that we are *kings* and *priests*. Hallelujah! Thank goodness we don't have to pick which one we are, but hypothetically, if for whatever strange reason we did had to pick and choose one or the other, which would you pick? Would you rather be *king* or *priest*?

Most of us would answer "king," of course.

Doesn't that go without saying?

Don't get me wrong, priests are cool, but... the king is the king. The king is the highest card in a deck. He commands the chessboard as well. Everything in our society screams "king." He makes the decisions, he sits in the giant cushioned chair, he is in front of the masses, he is the *leader*. It is the king who holds the royal scepter, whose head is adorned with a royal crown, who wields the power of a kingdom (it is called the "*king*dom," after all). The king is the king.

Consider even the worship songs we sing every Sunday morning and every Wednesday night. We never sing to Jesus as our "Great High Priest." No, He's the "King of Kings." He's the "Lord of Lords." The king is the top dog. Of course we'd choose king.

But not everyone would. Do you remember Saul, the ill-fated first king of Israel? He was chosen by God to lead the nation of Israel and reigned for many years, but his downfall was when he tried to offer sacrifices to God. Whose job was it to make the sacrifice? That would be the responsibility of the priest.

Uzziah became King of Judah many decades later and was a man who "did right in the sight of the Lord" and "sought God." However, later in life he too desired to be closer to God, to perform the duties of the priesthood. Then one day he stormed the temple in an attempt to burn incense to the Lord, and eighty priests linked arms and prevented him from entering into the Holiest of Holies.

King David himself desperately desired to stand in the office of the priest. If you read through his psalms you will see that over and over again he craved to burn incense to God, to dwell in the house of the Lord, to minister to his Savior.

There was just something about being a priest that made the king jealous. The priests were the ones who got to hang out with God all day. The word "priest" literally means, "draw near to God." The priests were invited to spend every waking minute of every single day at the feet of Yahweh, and in the nation of Israel that was a deeply coveted position.

But we don't think like that anymore. In today's day and age we want power. We want to rule. We want to be important. We want to be in charge. And for many, if seeking God is how we get into that position of comfortable power then we'll seek Him in order to gain access to His mighty power.

This last chapter I write to you as a warning to make sure you continue to walk *with* God rather than *ahead of* God. We've covered a lot of information in this book, a lot of which revolves around *you*. We've discussed extensively how awesome God has created you to be and how incredibly much God is willing to do for you. But as Stephen Colbert jokingly stated, "If a little knowledge is a dangerous thing, then *a lot* of knowledge is a *really* dangerous thing." I'm afraid that's true in this case. When you begin to see how God looks at you, it's very easy to take your eyes off of God and become focused on yourself. But understanding ourselves is exactly why we must keep our attention desperately fixed on Christ, for we are made in *His* image, and *He* is the source of the awesome existence we experience every day.

Monumental Events

The 103rd Psalm says that Israel knew God's works, but Moses knew God's ways. Now the works of God are amazing and spectacular and awesome. But God is more than the things He does. Think back to Martha and Mary, the friends of Jesus. Jesus came over for dinner one evening, and Martha labored tirelessly to prepare a delicious dinner for her Friend and Savior. After they finished the meal, Martha tidied up the house, washed all of the dishes, wrapped the leftovers in foil, and threw them in the fridge. While running around the house, cleaning this and vacuuming that, it occurred to her: *Where's Mary?*

She walked into the living room, and there was Mary, sitting at the feet of Jesus. Martha just about lost it. "Jesus, aren't you going to tell my lazy sister to come help me with all of this work?!"

Now if most of us were in Jesus' place we would have awkwardly offered to help, in order to avoid any further confrontation. Blessed are the peacemakers, after all. But Jesus reprimanded *Martha*. "There is something more important than the work you are doing, and Mary has found it."

It's important for us to do stuff, to serve others and to do those good works that God prepared for us to do. But we can never lose sight of God in the process. So many Christians serve a God they no longer know. Ministry has become their Lord, and Jesus is nowhere to be found. But listen closely. God wants you to love *Him*, not just love *serving Him*.

That bears repeating.

God wants you to love Him, not just love serving Him.

Don't get so caught up in the works that you miss God Himself. It's great to know God's works, but knowing God's ways is much, much better. How God moves, how God sounds, what God looks like, what God thinks. God Himself. Perfect peace. True joy. Overwhelming love. Utter perfection. *God.*

> *"One thing I have desired of the Lord, that will I seek: that I may dwell in the house of the Lord all the days of my life, to behold the beauty of the Lord, and to inquire in His temple."* (Psalm 27:4)

What a beautiful existence. To know nothing but God. Just to love, and be loved. To be *with* Love. To lose sight of everything around you. To be oblivious to circumstance and time and all things physical. To *know* God.

But a lot of people can't stand the thought of this existence, for there are too many things to be done. *We have that outreach program* on Saturday morning. After all, the sinners aren't going to save themselves*. And that is true. The lost must be reached. The gospel must be preached. But what good is it to save the world and lose your soul?

Flip through the gospels and you will find many "hidden" verses that we often overlook in our quest for purpose.

> "Now in the morning, having risen a long while before daylight, Jesus went out and departed to a solitary place; and there He prayed." (Mark 1:35)

> "So He Himself often withdrew into the wilderness and prayed." (Luke 5:16)

> "And when He had sent the multitudes away, He went up on the mountain by Himself to pray. Now when evening came, He was alone there." (Matthew 14:23)

> "Now it came to pass in those days that He went out to the mountain to pray, and continued all night in prayer to God." (Luke 6:12)

We read these passages and move on without giving them a second glance. But if you look at *when* these verses took place you would find that these seemingly insignificant occurrences all took place before and after major events in Jesus' ministry. The start of Jesus' ministry, healing the multitudes, calling the disciples, multiplying the loaves and fishes, walking on water, the crucifixion and resurrection… all these momentous events are bookended with fervent prayer and intimate worship.

It's easy to look at Jesus and see His life as one miracle after another, one sermon after another. In our understanding, the high points of His life seem to be the passionate teachings and mighty signs and wonders, and in between those cosmic events, things of lesser importance took place, like time spent with His Dad.

But what you have to recognize is that the high points of His life *were* those special moments spent with God, and throughout a life spent in constant and desperate communion with His Dad, Jesus happened to do other, less important things, like preach sermons and perform miracles.

Jesus didn't live a life of miracles. He lived a life with God, and miracles just started happening.

Jesus Himself, when discussing the miraculous, always gave the credit to His Dad.

> *"Then Jesus answered and said to them, 'Most assuredly I say to you, the Son can do nothing of Himself, but what He sees the Father do; for whatever He does, the Son also does in like manner.'" (John 5:19)*

Jesus explained the signs and wonders and miracles and mighty deeds quite simply. "I just spend time with God, and these things start happening." Your life should be one long walk with your heavenly Dad. You go where He goes. You say what He says. You do what He does. If your eyes are fixed on Him and your ears are bent in His direction, all doubt and worry will be removed. You'll just do what He says, and then the awesomeness will happen.

Then you can just continue walking with Him, without missing a step.

More than the Stuff

I want to finish with a final passage of scripture.

In the midst of the Sermon on the Mount, Jesus tells His church not to worry about food, or clothing, or shelter, or anything else. "God will take care of you," He assures them. Then He finishes the thought with this statement.

> *"'But seek first the kingdom of God and His righteousness, and all these things shall be added to you.'" (Matthew 6:33)*

In essence, don't worry about *stuff*. Whatever *stuff* you need, God will provide it. Just focus on Him. Unfortunately, this is what most Christians take away from that scripture:

> "I want the stuff, so I will seek God *first*. Then I can get the stuff."

But guess what? If your goal is to get the *stuff*, then you're not really seeking God first, now are you? In fact, for all intents and purposes, we should be able to read the verse this way.

> "But seek first the kingdom of God and His righteousness. Period."

And if you aren't just as content reading it that way, you're reading it wrong.

Don't get me wrong. The stuff is important. So are the miracles. And if you are in desperate need of a miracle, or even just in moderate need of one, there is nothing wrong with turning to God for help. That's why He made all of the fantastic promises He made. He promised provision, He promised healing, He promised overflowing joy and impossible peace and irresistible love. He promised to hear and answer every prayer you could ever muster up, simply because you are His delight. He'll do the stuff for you, no problem.

But the stuff and the miracles shouldn't get in the way of *Him*. He needs to be your first priority. He needs to be your deepest desire, your only source, your hope and joy and peace and faith. Your one true love. He's not the means by which we get what we need. He *is* what we need. And if He isn't your everything, you're doing this whole Christianity thing incorrectly.

I guess this is what I'm trying to say. God is more than the things He's done for you. He's more than the things He gives you. He's more than the healing He's provided for you or the prosperity He's given to you. He's more than signs and wonders and miracles. He's more than the Guy that handed out the Ten

Commandments and the Great Commission. Without all of that, He's still God. He's still good and perfect and mighty and awesome and amazing and spectacular and smart and cool and all-powerful and everything. He is *Everything*. Get that. *Everything*.

And as God, as your heavenly Dad, as the Eternal Ancient of Days, as the Almighty, everything else is handled. All of that *other stuff* falls into place. So don't fret. Not for a moment. Daddy's got it taken care of.

Yes, you're awesome and good and righteous. So is He. Let Him be your focus. Let Him be your delight. Let Him be God.

Small Group Questions

1. How does this chapter relate to what you're currently reading in the bible?

2. Would you rather be a king or a priest? Why?

3. Do you more related with Martha or with Mary? Why do you think that is?

4. What do you think Jesus would have considered His favorite moments in the gospels?

5. Why was Jesus able to do all of the amazing things He did?

6. What is more important than serving God?

7. Read Psalm 27:4. What is one notable thing about this verse?

8. What was the main point of this chapter?

Epilogue
Go

Go.

No, seriously. *Go*. Put the book down, and go change the world.

Go into every area of life, every business, every school, every park, every nation, every *place*, and preach the gospel. *Be* the gospel.

Heal the sick, cleanse the lepers, cast out the demons, raise the dead.

Feed the hungry, clothe the naked, care for the widows and orphans, be the light in this dark and dying world.

Help the helpless, defend the fatherless, speak up for those with no voice. Freely you have received. Freely give. To all those in need. To all those who ask.

Open the eyes of the blind and the ears of the deaf and the mouths of the dumb. Set the captives free, heal the broken hearts, throw open the prison gates, and as you go, boldly proclaim, "The kingdom of heaven is here!"

For that is true. The kingdom of heaven *is* here. Because *you* are here. You are an ambassador of the kingdom, a prince of heaven, a son of the Most High and a co-heir with Christ. And your commission, your mandate, your calling, should you choose to accept it, is to bring heaven to earth. To prevail over the gates of hell. To trample the enemy underfoot. To be fruitful. To multiply. To fill the earth. To make disciples of every nation, tribe, and tongue.

You are a history maker.
You are a world changer.
You are a culture shifter.
You are a life saver.

You are a kingdom giant.

So dream on, mighty man of God. Do the unexpected. See the unseeable. Venture into the unknowable. Step out of the boat and walk upon the crashing waves. *Be impossible.*

And as you head out into so great a destiny as lies before you, remember that God, the mighty *Elohim* who fashioned galaxies and daisies and mountains and supernovas, who holds the entire universe in the palm of His hand, who at this very moment is keeping gravity tugging and the sun rising and the stars shining and yet still manages to put breath in your lungs, *The* God, is with you. He is *in* you. He will never leave you. He will never forsake you. Even to the ends of the earth. Even to the ends of time.

And there is *nothing* that can separate you from Him. Absolutely nothing. Not your past, not your present, not your future, not good things nor bad, not the angels nor the demons nor principalities nor powers nor heavenly hosts nor any created thing. *Nothing* can take you away from the overwhelming love He is pouring out all over you.

And if God is with you, who can stand against you? If God be for you, who *cares* who's against you? If God is on your side, case closed. It's settled. The end.

You are more than a conqueror. You can do *all* things. You really do have an unfair advantage. It's so unfair it's not even funny. The game is totally rigged in your favor. And you will win.

You are greater than you realize.

So *go*, take the world by storm.

The devil doesn't stand a chance.

About Garrett

Garrett Milovich is a Christian teacher and writer who has preached both nationally and internationally. He lives in Orange County with his wife Cheyne and son Jack. Together they oversee the youth and young adult ministries at their local church.

In addition to spending exorbitant amounts of time talking about God and the bible, Garrett spends his free time hiking, writing stories and songs for his son, embarrassing his wife in public, seeing midnight showings of superhero movies, traveling the world with his family, solving difficult math problems, playing laser-tag with "his boys," skeet shooting, creating iPhone apps, hosting various outreaches in the community, directing short films, and discussing the inner workings of time travel as seen in the *Terminator* films.

For more from Garrett Milovich, check out his website at **GarrettMilovich.com**. To request Garrett to speak at your church or event, email us at **Garrett@GarrettMilovich.com**.

Like what you read?
Post your favorite quotes on
Facebook, *Instagram*, and *Twitter*!
Remember to hashtag
#UnfairAdvantageBook!

Made in the USA
San Bernardino, CA
27 May 2018